LISTENING BOOK 4

*20-Minute Exercises to Add Variety
To Your Riding Routine*

Kathy Farrokhzad

Photographs by Jackie Boesveld

Illustration by Jeff Thompson

*A COLLECTION OF ARTICLES FROM
HORSE LISTENING: THE BLOG*

Horse Listening Book 4: 20-Minute Exercises To Add Variety To Your Riding Routine
Copyright © 2018 by Kathy Farrokhzad.
All Rights Reserved.

All rights reserved. No part of this book may be reproduced in any form or by any electronic or mechanical means including information storage and retrieval systems, without permission in writing from the author.

Cover designed by Kathy Farrokhzad

Visit my website at www.horselistening.com

First Printing: December 2018
Full Circle Equestrian
P.O. Box 30033, Oakville, ON L6H 6Y0

ISBN-13 978-1-9995616-0-4 (Paperback)
ISBN-13 978-1-9995616-1-1 (Ebook)

DEDICATION

K. Arbuckle: For being literally the "Quality Control" person for all of my patterns and exercises, and even more importantly, for all your expertise and support especially over the past four years.

J. Boesveld: For your unwavering kindness and encouragement, and for taking these top quality photos!

SAFETY FIRST

In all of this book's chapters, as in all riding, concern for the horse's well-being, health and longevity is at the forefront of our efforts. It is also the method behind the madness of all the suggestions in this book.

As with all physical endeavors, horseback riding requires a certain level of fitness, balance and coordination. The unpredictable nature of the horse always adds an element of uncertainty and danger that we need to be aware of.

Please use any and all of the suggestions in this book at your discretion. Feel free to change anything to meet the needs of you and your horse. Finally, be sure to "listen" because the horse will always let you know if you are on the right track.

CONTENTS

SAFETY FIRST ix
INTRODUCTION xiii
PRE-AMBLE.. 1
1. Eleven Unexpected Side-Benefits Of Riding Tests (Or Patterns)............ 3
2. Why We Dressage: The Rider 9
3. Why We Dressage: The Horse 13
SECTION 1: WARM-UPS... 17
4. Exercise: A Simple And Effective Horse Riding Warm-Up 19
5. What "In Front Of The Leg" Feels Like 25
6. The Essential Open Rein 29
7. An Awesome Over-The-Back Suppling Warm-Up At The Walk........... 34
8. How To Stretch Your Horse Over The Top Line 38
9. Walking The WALK In Horse Riding 43
SECTION 2: LEFT AND RIGHT.. 47
10. How To Change Directions In The Riding Ring 49
11. What Bend Really Means.. 55
12. "Inside Leg To Outside Rein" – The Cheat Sheet................................. 59
13. Six Steps To A Well-Balanced Change Of Direction 64
14. What Is Contact?.. 69

    The First Stage: "Take Up" The Contact 70
    The Second Stage: "On The Bit"... 72
    The Third Stage: "On The Aids" Or "Connection" 75

15. Where Does Your Half-Halt Start? Here Are Four Suggestions......... 80
SECTION 3: STRAIGHTNESS 85
16. Straight Line To Turn Off The Rail (The Tear Drop) 87
17. The Power of Straightness – And A Checklist 90
18. What Is A Neck Bend? And What To Do About It 95
FOCUS ON TRANSITIONS 99
I. The Five Stages Of A Transition 101
II. Week 1... 106
III. Week 2 114
IV. Week 3 119
V. Week 4 123

VI. The Simple (?) Halt To Walk Transition 127
VII. A Transition Exercise To Jazz Up Your Riding Routine 132
VIII. Lighten Your Horse's Forehand – From the Hind End 136
IX. Seven Essential Aids For An Epic Canter Transition 141
X. How To Fine-Tune Your Canter-Trot Transitions 147
XI. A Stretch And Strengthen Canter Exercise 151
XII. Bold Transitions That Look Effortless and Feel Great 156
SECTION 4: SUPPLENESS 161
19. Leg Yield/ Shoulder-Fore – A Great Way To Your Horse's Back...................... 163
20. Go With The Horse 168
21. Three Steps To A Quieter Leg Position 172
22. Suppling Fun! An Exercise 177
23. Thirty-Eight Moments To Half-Halt.. 183
24. Get Rid of That Tension: Four Steps To Improved Suppleness 187
SECTION 5: COLLECTION..191
25. The Many Uses Of The Oval 193
26. Crystal Clear About Canter Leads & A Quick Fix 198
27. What To Do When Your Horse Pulls 203
28: Collection: A Beginning Exercise To Try 207
29. The Benefits Of Cantering Round And Round The Ring 213
30. How A Simple 1,2,1,2... Can Improve Your Ride 217
PARTING THOUGHTS 223
31. Three Relaxing Ways To Cool Down At The End Of Your Ride 225
32. The Difference Between Rhythm and Tempo 229
33. Why Boring Is Beautiful In Horse Back Riding 234
34. "You're STILL Taking Riding Lessons?" 237
35. 10 Symptoms Of A Horse-A-Holic 240
36. The Truth About Perfect Practice And The HL Rider Learning Cycle 244
37. Twenty-Four Reasons Why Horsin' Around Makes Us Better Human Beings
.... 249
ABOUT THE AUTHOR... 253

INTRODUCTION

The exercises in this book are timeless. ☺

How do I know? Because I've been using them for years, with riders and horses at various levels, and for myself while riding my own horses and client horses. You'll see that there are different types of exercises included in this book, from patterns that focus on straight lines, to others that work with only circles, and to still more than work on developing better suppleness and balance.

These exercises might not be what you might expect from a dressage-type text. They are not organized in a sequential, do-this-first and only do the next one after mastering the first one, order. In my practice, I have learned to recognize that each day might be different, each ride might bring on a new challenge, and you should be prepared with a variety of ideas that can help make that ride successful.

Many dressage masters and top trainers talk about having this sort of fluidity in your riding expectations and plans. My own horse, Cyrus, is a perfect example of day-to-day variety. I have to be an open, "listening" rider, because in the end, the ride isn't as much about me as it is about him. While I constantly recognize that I have to improve my own skills in order to make myself a better rider, I have also learned that I need to meet him where he's at on that particular day.

This is actually where the whole concept of Horse "Listening" came from. If we aren't "whispering" to our horses, then what are we really doing? And for me, it's all about Listening.

Now, Listening doesn't mean that I should sit back and do nothing with the horses. Quite the opposite! It's more about creating intentional goals, identifying how I can achieve those goals, and *then recognizing where the horse is and what I need to do to meet his needs.* I mean, I might have a long-term goal of showing next season, but if Cyrus isn't anywhere near ready physically or mentally, then we're not going. It's as simple as that. And it's my job to figure out what I need to do to take him to that goal, step by step, day to day. And to be patient enough to wait.

This is where these riding exercises come in. One day, Cyrus might be sluggish and less active in the hind end. That day, I'll likely choose the straighter, more forward exercises, to get him to become better engaged, more forward and ahead of the leg, and generally better over the back. We jazz up those rides!

Another day, he might be wound up and excited. That day, he's fully able to come from behind with a possibly over-active hind! Then I'll pull out the circle patterns, so that they help keep his enthusiasm under control, use that energy to bring his inside hind leg underneath more (and develop better engagement), and work on better balance and bend.

Day to day, we build on what we've done, recognize where we are, and start there. Then we take it one step further before ending the ride.

While I recommend that you use these patterns regularly, I think you should pick and choose between them to pinpoint particular goals and needs as you go through your riding journey with your horse.

I've added relevant chapters of theory, or quality of movement exercises, in-between the main patterns. This way, you can plan on an exercise and have follow-up thoughts and ideas supporting it.

Try to do these exercises over 20 minutes or so. The idea is to repeat them enough so that both you and your horse have a chance to practice enough to make some improvement over each ride. Make sure you do the exercises on both reins.

All of the *Horse Listening Collection* books have one main underlying theme: to develop and then build on success for the sake of the horse. This book continues that intention.

Success might mean something completely different from person to person, and horse to horse. But underneath it all, there are a few core principles that guide us toward that success.

First, above all else, be safe. Stay aware of the circumstance and environment around you, and be ever vigilant to reduce unnecessary risks. You can always tone down the ride and come back to your intended lesson another day. Safety is key for both you and your horse. Stay calm and make progress through patience.

Second, aim to be a lifelong learner. As horse people, we often fall victim to presenting ourselves ego-first to our fellow horse lovers. Seek education – from clinics, horse professionals (vets, horse nutritionists, massage therapists, and all of the other experts that make themselves available for the horse's health), backyard owners, riding instructors, books, and yes, even the increasingly amazing free videos that are now posted on the Internet! There is no longer any excuse to not be able to find the information you need when you need it.

Finally, practice. Keep developing your skills. It has been said that it takes many lifetimes to learn everything that can be learned about, with, and for horses. So get on it! The better your skills, the better you can communicate to your horse, whether riding or on the ground. While most of us will not be heading to the Olympics, we sure can stay on that self-improvement path for the sake of our horses.

Because in the end, it's all about the horses!

PRE-AMBLE

1. ELEVEN UNEXPECTED SIDE-BENEFITS OF RIDING TESTS (OR PATTERNS)

Turn left here. Canter circle there. Halt for five seconds. Then trot in a straight line out of the halt.

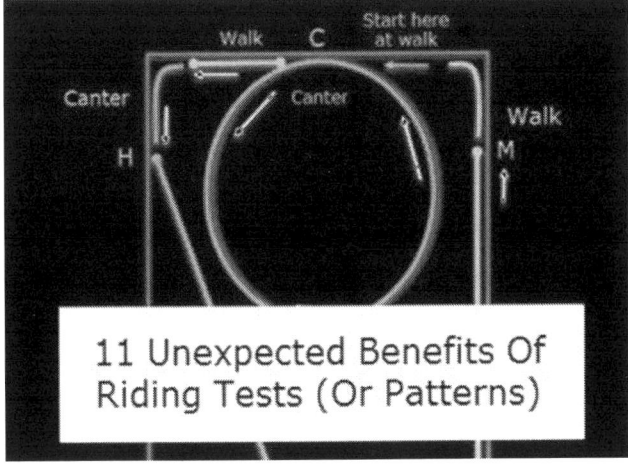

If you've never ridden tests (or patterns - I'll use the word "test" for simplicity here) before, you might be in for a bit of a surprise. You gotta do what you gotta do when you're told to do it! There's no built-in sensitivity to your horse's tendency to trot before the canter transition. Your squiggly "straight" line might become a lot more apparent when it's supposed to be off the rail down center line. Or you might become more aware of your horse's lean-through-the-corner-and-fall-off-the-rail just before you need to set up for a lengthen at trot.

When we ride on our own, or even in a lesson, we tend to ride according to our needs (both the rider and the horse). We take time to develop our transitions, ride half a circle or even more to increase impulsion, half-halt the balance to allow better rounding through the horse's body, maybe increase impulsion a little more... then *finally* proceed with the transition.

To be sure, this is *the* way to improve our skills. Learning takes time, and developing accurate aids and responses from the horse takes practice. There are occasions when there simply is no other way, and rushing yourself or your horse results in stress and tension and maybe even worse.

However, there is something to be said about putting yourself through tests or patterns. If you rarely ride a pattern, you might initially be surprised how difficult it can be to ride according to specifications. But it is very much worth the effort.

There are so many side-benefits to practicing a test.

Even while you are working on one part, so many other things have to fall together to make the test flow. Check them out below!

1. Focus on specifics

When you work on particular movements, you realize how much goes into each skill. For example, a lengthen at canter down the rail may look like the horse just took larger, bounding strides. But give it a try and you'll notice that developing the lengthen through the body takes more than just energy.

The tempo needs to be maintained while the impulsion is increased. Keeping the line straight looks a lot easier than it feels, especially if your horse has a tendency to lean on a shoulder!

2. Become more consistent

When you ride movement to movement, you become more aware of the lurches and stop-starts that happen during each figure. Have you ever noticed your horse lose energy going into a corner? Or maybe he shortens his stride length as he steps into the beginning of a circle. Test riding will help you notice inconsistencies and give you reason to work on them.

3. Accurate transitions

In dressage tests, you ride movements letter to letter. It happens in other disciplines too, where the patterns indicate exactly where a gait or figure begins and ends. When you are not used to being accurate, you let the horse take those few extra strides before or after a given point. Working on specific placements of transitions makes you and your horse sharper and more in tune with each other.

4. Well ridden figures

Once you know the test, you also learn the exact dimensions of a figure. Let's take a loop, for example. The loop starts at the letter after the corner, goes to X and then back to the final letter before the next corner. Following set figures gives you and your horse a reason to develop specific abilities, such as changing bends, stepping deeper underneath the body, maintaining rhythm and tempo, and so much more.

5. Count strides

When you stick to what you are required to do in a test, you will learn a lot about your horse. One thing you might notice is the stride length your horse may have for each particular movement. You might realize, for example, that your horse takes 4 strides from the last letter into the corner. This information could help you in the timing of your half-halts and bends into and out of each corner.

6. Improve your aids

You'll have to get better at your aids in order to be more accurate. So as you practice, you'll find what you need to adjust - maybe an outside leg here, an inside weighted seat there. You'll recognize how to be a more active rider and predict problems before they arise, in order to fulfill the requirements of the test.

7. Develop bend and straightness

These two wonderful concepts are easy to forget or become lazy about in general. When you aren't carefully placing movements according to a sequence, you tend to let the horse go a bit straighter (or even counter bent) on a bend, or a little over bent on a line. Haunches to the inside, anyone?

8. Be more comfortable during stress

There is no doubt that having to do particular movements in particular places adds a stress element to both the horse and rider. Once in a while, it is good to work within that stress level to develop the ability to continue to perform even under less than perfect conditions. It will get better with practice.

9. Learn new skills

Do you ever get caught in a rut of doing the same thing over and over again? Use the tests to encourage you to learn new movements you may have forgotten about or never attempted. The dressage tests, in particular, are leveled in a way that you can work from one test to the next, as they increase in difficulty. This way, you never stagnate at one point for very long.

10. Think ahead

When you ride movement to movement, something wonderful happens pretty much on its own. Even while you are performing one figure, you need to know what is coming next so you can set up for it. Thinking ahead while riding is an excellent way to develop a flow to your riding that you can't achieve when you do one thing at a time.

11. Look where you're going

Do you tend to look down when you ride? You won't have that opportunity when you need to plan where you are going in the test! You must look to the letters, to the perimeters of the ring, and to the placement of the figures, so eyes come up naturally.

If you dedicate some time to practicing tests on a regular basis, you will notice improvement in your ability to meet the predetermined goals of each test. As you become more familiar, you can start to work on new skills that challenge you to grow and develop – both horse and rider.

2. WHY WE DRESSAGE: THE RIDER

Dressage (in French) = To Train
It stands to reason, then, that all horse riders should learn dressage, even while specializing in their chosen discipline. I'm not talking about the type of dressage that it takes to get into a show ring well enough to put down a great score (which isn't a bad thing to do for sure), but the kind that teaches riders fundamental skills that are the basis of all good movement.

This is not to say that different riding disciplines don't teach effective skills. Far from it. But because dressage training is rooted in the absolute basics that all horses will go through (whether or not the riders are aware), time spent on developing the dressage in the rider is never wasted! Dressage can be a powerful addition to your regular riding program.

ALL disciplines use circles, straight lines, suppleness, transitions, energy from the hind end, and more. ALL riders can benefit from learning how to use their aids effectively, even if they ride in different tack with a different body position. Because in the end, "all horses have a head, a tail and four legs - and gravity sucks the same way for all of them!" (*credit for that quote goes to my long time awesome dressage instructor)

Here is what dressage can do for you, the rider.

1. Education

Let's start with the main reason. Riders from all disciplines will benefit from the fundamental instruction that is rooted in dressage. There is a reason that terms and phrases such as "inside leg to outside rein," "forward," and "hind end engagement" are pervasive in all riding arenas. While they are technically taught in dressage, they are applicable to all sorts of riding activities.

Riders who have spent some time learning the dressage basics will always have those skills to inform their future endeavors. Many riders from various disciplines use dressage techniques in their daily riding activities - not to take to the dressage ring, but to take to *their* preferred ring. Knowing what to do, why and when to use a technique or skill can make a huge difference in both the short and long term success of the rider.

2. Seat Use

When you hear "dressage," you probably instantly think "seat." The whole concept of using the seat as the beginning and end of balance, communication and "aiding" is a core teaching of dressage. When riders lack an educated seat, they likely spend their rides being reactive, out of balance, and ultimately, on the ground after an unplanned dismount.

Learning to use the seat effectively takes years of practice and is one of those things that you never stop developing, but every horse will benefit from your dressage-acquired seat.

3. Independent Aids

Another main component of dressage is to get riders to use their aids independently of each other. So when the seat is balancing or asking for more engagement, the hands are not pulling but still adequately containing the energy that is delivered to them. The elbows might be soft but toned while the hands are closed and not letting the reins out. The seat does its job while the legs stay inactive and on the horse's sides until more energy is required.

It takes a considerable amount of coordination to be able to work each body part independently from the other, but it can be done.

4. Connection/Contact

Dressage riders spend a large amount of time on both contact and connection, and for good reason. Communication with the horse is critical in all endeavors and the way we communicate can make or break a horse's life. Many riding problems and even lamenesses can be corrected by achieving "connection" - that amazing feeling of the looseness of a horse that is moving confidently forward into your rein contact and responding to your subtle aids despite the great energy he is offering.

This is another life-long quest that can be beneficial to all disciplines.

5. Quality Movement

Movement is another essential part of dressage - but in reality, it is necessary for any kind of horse related activity. Movement is what we're all after, and *good* gaits are desired in all riding styles, whether it be under saddle, in harness or at liberty. You'd be amazed at how much an educated rider can influence the quality of their horse's movement.

Dressage concepts are extremely relevant for all horses and disciplines. Adding a little dressage into your regular riding routine can make a huge difference in the level of success in your chosen field. Don't take my word for it. Just listen to your horse!

3. WHY WE DRESSAGE: THE HORSE

While most people think of the competition ring when they hear the word "dressage," there is so much more to be gained from the system of dressage than originally might meet the eye. I mean, it's only walk, trot and canter (with the occasional lateral movement thrown in), right?

But there is a secret about dressage. Because the focus, especially at the lower levels, is on developing quality movement, there is much to be gained for riders of other disciplines to learn and then develop these skills in their horses. Which discipline *doesn't* want the horse to move as well as it can?

So here are 11 reasons why we dressage the horse.

1. The Path

First off, the dressage "levels" and the training scale give riders a well thought-out path to follow when training their horse. While not everyone aims to compete, the organization of all the skills into levels allows every rider to follow a sequential order of progression, from the very basic to the advanced. It's not all about the horse, either. Rider's skills are also progressively addressed so that the rider can effectively influence (and balance) the horse.

2. Inside Hind Leg

You might hear somewhat of an obsession about the inside hind leg among dressage enthusiasts. There is good reason for this. When we ride a horse in the ring, the inside hind leg carries the balance of the horse. The inside hind leg that can step deeper underneath the horse will always be able to carry the horse and rider's weight better, maintain a better rhythm and tempo, and use the musculature of the horse's body in a way that allows the horse to move stronger with less constraint.

3. Swinging Back

The back is another area of obsession because without a supple and swinging back, the horse will always move in tension and rigidity. Done over the long term, the tightness of the horse's back transfers to every part of the horse's body, and can eventually be the root cause of a variety of lamenesses. And so... we try and try some more to move with the horse, and allow the energy "through".

4. Rider Education

Dressage isn't all about the horse, of course (well, it is, really). Because if the rider doesn't know how to create these flowing, going movements, even the kindest, most accommodating horse will inevitably suffer. And so in order to dressage the horse, we need to dressage the rider too.

5. Rider Position and Effectiveness

The rider can look "pretty" on the horse, but in order for the *horse* to look pretty, there must be more than just holding the body in a certain way. And so in dressage, you will get into "the effectiveness of the rider," because without that, the movement will always suffer, even in the most talented horse.

6. Quietness of Aids

One of the most common observations about good dressage riding is that it looks like the rider is doing nothing; the horse is just moving merrily along and the rider moves not an inch! Well, if you know riding at all, you'll know that the quieter the rider looks, the more work she has done to get to that place. We're talking about muscle memory, coordination, balance, timing, and so much more. And it's not really that the rider wants to appear motionless - it's more that the rider wants to become "at one" with the horse - the ultimate place to be!

7. Suppleness

Nowhere will you hear the word "suppleness" more than in the dressage ring. This is because in order for the horse to be able to do anything with ease, he has to learn to flex left and right, and over the top line. This is something that needs to be learned early and then maintained as the horse becomes more fit and educated. All horses, in all disciplines, benefit from suppleness.

8. Transitions

In dressage, we live in transitions! And transitions help the horse with engagement, impulsion, and all the good things that come from reaching deeper underneath the body with the hind legs. Transitions also get the horse and rider tuned into each other, helping to develop better communication and responsiveness between them.

9. Power From The Hind End

You simply can't "dressage" the horse without working on increasing the power of the hind end. The stronger the horse can become in the hind end, the better he will maneuver through his discipline-specific movements.

10. Off The Forehand

The reason we want the horse's hind end to strengthen is so that he can learn to "balance back" - and take some of that weight off the forehand. The fit and balanced horse is much better able to carry the rider. He also puts much less weight on to the front legs and shoulders.

11. Dancing

Finally, this is where the magic happens! Because once all the above areas are developed, the horse and rider will have the skills and relationship to play at will. And this is what riding is all about.

SECTION 1: WARM-UPS

4. EXERCISE: A SIMPLE AND EFFECTIVE HORSE RIDING WARM-UP

I've written about warm-ups before but this is one of my favorites.

I often start the ride with this exercise, and it's great for so many reasons! It suits many horses for different end goals. Of course, you can use it during the middle of the ride as well, or maybe even make this your whole ride with a few variations. This warm-up is suitable for:
- young horses
- inexperienced older horses
- the sluggish to start horse
- the runaway to start horse (!)
- the imbalanced horse
- the horse that is still trying to find a good tempo and rhythm
- the horse working on basic gaits and transitions.

Kathy Farrokhzad

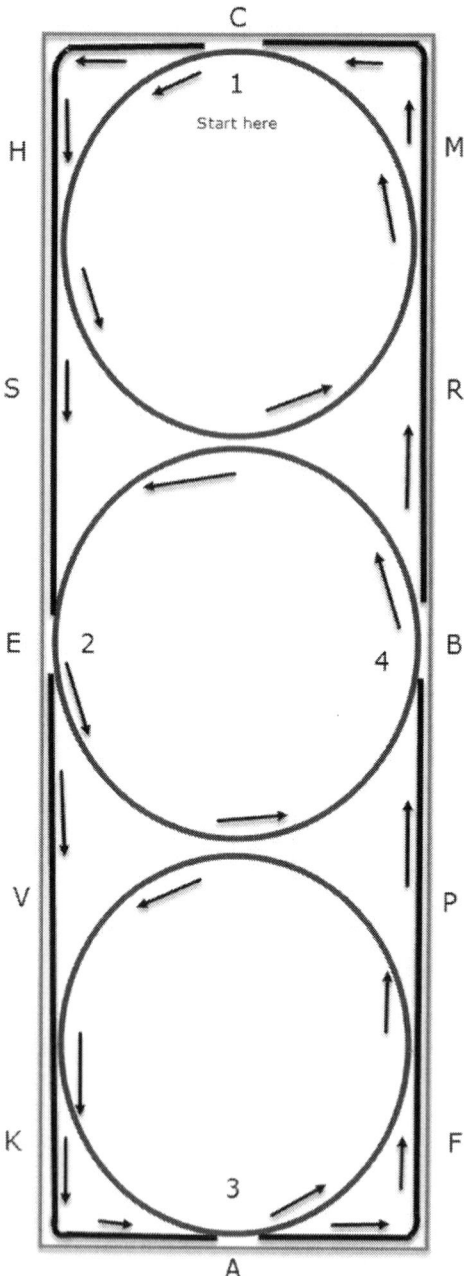

It is also useful for:
- the young rider
- the inexperienced rider
- the rider who is working on basic aids
- the rider who wants to find a good rhythm and tempo
- the rider who is nervous of the runaway or unpredictable horse
- the rider who needs some structure in the warm-up.

♦ ♦ ♦

The actual exercise is fairly simple (but beware: simple may not be easy). Basically, you do four 20-meter circles as you make your way around the ring once.

Start at C (Circle #1). If I'm on the left rein, I will start at trot and do a 20-metre circle at C. Then I'll navigate the corner, and head up the rail to E.

Go into a new 20-metre circle (#2) at E. Then back to the rail, the corner, and head to A.

Start a new circle (#3) at A. Complete that circle, go to the corner, and head for B.

This first round ends with a final circle (#4) at B. Go back to the track and head to A again.

I'll use this figure at the walk for ten minutes or so before I start the trot. Once I'm in the trot, I'll work on developing a strong but steady trot through the whole figure.

You can also do this at the canter of course, which presents all kinds of new and exciting challenges as you navigate turns and straight lines.

Do it several times each way, at each gait.
Pay particular attention to the following.
Circle Size and Placement
You don't have to aim for exact 20-meter circles if you are not practicing for dressage tests. However, do pick a circle size that fits your riding space, and be consistent all the way around the ring. Make it even on both sides (avoid falling in or drifting out).

Flexion
Flexion is one of the most basic component of suppleness over the top line. Always work on getting your horse to look in the direction of movement. You don't even have to pretzel into a bend on these circles because of their large size.

However, you should be able to see the corner of your horse's inside eye in the turns. This helps your horse release the tension especially in the jaw and neck, as well as position him for better balance through a turn.

Rhythm and Tempo
This one is for the less-than-inspired horses and conversely, for the runaways. Try to find your horse's ideal tempo and stick to it.

Make sure it is energetic enough to allow him to use his hindquarters in such a way that he will have better balance in the turns and circles. You may need to jazz up the energy a bit in the circles - many horses tend to slow down or disengage when they head into a turn.

On the other hand, if your horse just goes faster-faster-faster, the circles are a great natural vehicle to help you regulate that leg speed and balance the horse better to the hind end. Use plenty of half-halts before, through and after each circle and in the corners.

Straightness

This figure alternates between mild bends on the circles, and straightness on the rails. This helps teach you and your horse to straighten after a bend and bend after being straight.

The straight lines give your horse a chance to unwind a bit out of the circles, reach forward and energize, and prepare for the next corner or turn. If your horse has a tendency to ride with his shoulders close to the rail, you might want to do a shoulder-fore as you travel up the straight lines.

Balance

As already mentioned, this exercise is a study in balance. Your horse might fall in to the circle. He might drift out. He might fall to the forehand on the straight lines. He might speed up and slow down. He might turn his neck in too much, or have a crooked head position.

These are all symptoms of imbalance and can be improved with half-halts, transitions and impulsion. As you develop your feel, you will know when to add some energy, when to stop it from "running out the front end", and when to slow the feet down altogether.

It is quite a challenge to be able to keep your horse in balance, in rhythm, in a steady tempo that is energetic but not too fast, in a mild bend as you go into and out of circles and lines. In fact, it is challenging enough that I tend to use this for not only beginner horses or riders, but also for the more advanced ones as they find their way through the nuances that improve quality of gait, connectedness and harmony. I use it myself too for horses at all stages.

Finally, you can get more creative with this figure. Once you feel you have a good handle on it, you can play around with transitions or circle sizes. You can canter one circle, trot another, walk a corner. The sky is the limit in terms of what you can add to make it more exciting!

5. WHAT "IN FRONT OF THE LEG" FEELS LIKE

"**K**eep the horse in front of your leg!" This is an expression you might often hear in dressage lessons, but it is also highly relevant and often referred to in other disciplines. Although the phrase sounds fairly self-explanatory, knowing what it feels like can be difficult to ascertain especially when you're just learning.

What It Isn't

"In front of the leg" isn't just faster. Even though there is a significant energy increase when the horse increases the tempo of the footfalls, speed isn't exactly what you're looking for. If you could harness the energy you get from speeding up, but *not* let the legs move faster, then you'll be on the right track.

It also isn't so strong that your horse is gets heavier on the reins and falls to the forehand. Even if you can increase the energy without leg speed, you shouldn't end up having so much energy forward that it causes your horse to fall out of balance.

To avoid this "throwing of the energy out the front end," you need to use effective half-halts that help keep the energy harnessed so that the horse can use it to improve everything from balance to quality of movement.

What It Feels Like

You can probably identify what "in front of the leg" looks like, but here we will focus on the feel, because when you're riding, you don't always have the privilege of knowing how you appear (although a friend with a video camera or mirrors in your riding area can be indispensable for your progress).

There's no stop to the movement

Do you know how it feels when your horse wants to stop every step of the way? You end up almost trotting or cantering *for* your horse, constantly using your legs or pumping your seat just to get that next stride?

That is the opposite of what "in front of the leg" feels like. When your horse is going well, you feel like the energy is just there. Your horse trots along until you ask for a transition. He canters and allows you to communicate with him during the canter - half-halt here, turn there, stay balanced here, lengthen there. So rather than using all your attention to keeping him going, you can focus on other things and count on him to maintain the gait.

The energy is rhythmical and forward

One of the first hints to "in front of the leg" is rhythm. If the horse wants to stop every other stride, you simply won't be able to maintain a clear rhythm or tempo of the footfalls. So that should be your first focus.

But then, there is also this sense of forward energy, the kind that feels like the horse is moving under his own power. You both progress ahead in space together freely and with regularity. It's not fast but it's also not restricted. He feels like he'll explode forward at a moment's notice, with the slightest leg aid.

Good balance

A horse that is in front of the leg is also in balance. There is a purely physical reason for this. When the horse is forward and rhythmical (without falling to the forehand), the inside hind leg reaches further underneath the body and promotes better balance.

You'll find that your horse has an easier time with everything from transitions to changes of direction, but done well, you might also feel your horse actually lighten on the forehand and assume an uphill tendency in the front end.

Round movement

Along with energy and balance, you'll find your horse can "round" easier. So instead of feeling like a piece of plywood through the back and neck, you should feel that the horse can send the energy "over the back" and allow longitudinal flexion to occur.

A gentle half-halt can result in the hind end rounding so the legs step deeper, the back assuming more of a "bridge" that can carry the weight of the rider and the poll and jaw softening in response to the bit contact.

The horse's neck is thick at the base

I think of this as a "stallion neck." Even though your horse may not be a stallion, the freely energetic horse can allow enough energy through the body so that the base of the neck is elevated slightly into this gorgeous neck arch position that bulges with muscles and looks surprisingly thick.

Expressive movement

Your horse's movement simply becomes more expressive. Rather than moving flat and uninspired, the horse that is in front of the leg moves with animation, eagerness and buoyancy. His ears might be slightly forward (not like in a spook), because he is looking ahead and thinking forward.

Bold and Confident

Finally, the horse exudes a boldness and confidence that is simply not present otherwise. The horse moves forward, straight ahead between the legs and reins, seeming to know exactly where he is going and what he is going to do. The sense of confidence allows for a certain level of "looseness" or lack of tension.

If you're not used to riding a horse that is "in front of the leg," you might be somewhat unnerved at first at the strength and energy that forms every stride. You might even get left behind a bit, as your upper body and core must become more adept at keeping up with the horse's movement.

But the rewards are exhilarating. While your horse moves along, you are free to work on yourself. You are also able to use your aids more effectively to improve your communication with your horse - a goal we aspire to work toward at all times.

6. THE ESSENTIAL OPEN REIN

Depending on whom you talk to, the open rein may be considered the "go to" aid, or the one rein aid with the bad rap. Many people move onto more sophisticated rein aids fairly soon in their riding process, convinced that the open rein is only for the young or the inexperienced.

The thing is, this rein aid is like the letter "a" in the alphabet. You simply can't start reading without knowing how it works and what it can do. Even when you become a fully mature, experienced reader, you can't just drop that letter in favor of all the others. It's always there, ready to be used in different ways, in a variety of circumstances.

And so it goes with the open rein.

What is the open rein?

It's the simplest, most basic rein aid we learn. It is of course useful in all the disciplines and with all types of bridles because of its primary effect, which is to invite the horse into the open space created by the rein action.

To open the rein, you simply move it away from the horse's neck, in the intended direction. Note that you don't pull back while you open. The pressure on the rein should be the same as it was when your hand was close to the neck. Your elbow should still be on your side as usual (i.e. don't open your elbow in the direction as well - no "chicken wings!"). The opening comes from your forearm as it moves away from the horse's neck.

The rein should be only 4 to 6 inches off the horse's neck. It doesn't need to open wide, or for you to take your hand to your knee (however tempting that may be at times). In fact, as you get better at opening the rein, you can reduce the distance from the horse's neck. Most advanced horse and riders can find the smallest open rein as useful as a wide one. Think maybe 2 inches off the neck as you progress in your balance and aids.

It sounds so simple, right? Just like the letter "a". Once you know the sounds (short and long a), you're ready to read every word it's used in!

Till you come across the more complicated words!

There's more to it than that.

So here's the thing with the open rein. Although that rein is fairly simple, it can't happen on its own. There have to be supporting aids that go along with it. While you're working on the one rein, you have to coordinate your seat, outside rein and leg aids *at the same time.*

Otherwise, you will accomplish little. The only thing that happens if you use the open rein in isolation is that you literally turn the horse's nose in the direction of the pressure. He may or may not follow that pressure (has your horse ever moved in the *opposite* direction of the rein aid?). He may swing his neck in the direction and lose his straightness. He may also lose balance and engagement.

So in reality, the open rein isn't for the faint hearted!

When can you use an open rein?

Here are five common situations in which you could use an open rein to encourage better balance, throughness, impulsion and suppleness, depending on the situation. I'll start at the beginning for a beginner rider and horse, and then develop into more advanced use.

1. New Rider

The new rider clearly benefits from learning the open rein. As hand-dominated human beings, we are always pointing toward the objects of our attention. One of the most intuitive ways to learn to direct a horse is to essentially "point" with the rein. Open the rein to the direction you want to move in, and the better educated horse will comply.

However, you should also use your entire body and outside rein to support the open rein.

2. Young or Uneducated Horse

The open rein is one of the first rein aids a young horse will learn, even if more developed rein aids are introduced shortly thereafter.

Used with the supporting aids from the rider's body, the open rein will teach the horse that pressure on the mouth translates into movement in a direction. It is an uncomplicated aid and naturally invites the horse to step into the opening created by the rein.

3. Straighten the Outside Shoulder

Does your horse have a tendency to "fall in" to the turn or circle? This means that when you turn, the horse cuts the circle toward the inside of the ring, thereby not really staying on the arc of the circle at all. You are lucky that your great seat can follow his trajectory, otherwise, you would continue on the circle (horseless) while he heads off somewhere completely different!

In this instance, the *outside* open rein can act as a correction.

A slight open rein on the outside will invite the outside shoulder to stay where it is and prevent it from falling in. In effect, you're creating some space to help encourage the shoulder to stay on the arc of the circle (straight on the circle). This is straightness.

You also need a direct inside rein (the rein that goes straight from the horse's mouth to your elbow, parallel to the horse's neck) as a support. This rein will also help to keep the horse's head from turning completely to the outside.

4. Invite Flexion

A mild open rein will invite the horse to turn his head just enough for you to be able to see the corner of his inside eye. That way, he will be looking in the direction of travel. Flexion is the beginning of softening of the poll, throughness and maintaining balance.

The inside open rein, coupled with an outside direct or neck rein (depending on if the horse is on a straight line or on a turn) will encourage the horse to flex to the inside. Flexion is the beginning of bend, so with the correct seat and leg aids, you can progress to bend as the horse becomes more educated.

5. Shift Weight to The Outside

This is the most complicated use of the open rein, and follows flexion.

Using an inside open rein (and outside rein as described above), and an active inside seat bone and leg, you can actually ask the horse to *step out*, away from the opening rein. This can be very helpful when you want to shift the horse's weight off the inside shoulder, and initiate a flexion or bend at the same time.

It also allows the horse to learn to step straight through with the inside shoulder rather than fall in or duck toward the middle of the ring (similar to #3 above, but focusing on the inside shoulder instead). A straight inside shoulder can be a big help when it comes to allowing the energy through the body - which means improved impulsion, throughness and suppleness.

Photo: N. Banaszak

7. AN AWESOME OVER-THE-BACK SUPPLING WARM-UP AT THE WALK

I've been using this exercise as a warm-up for both myself and my horse lately and I'm seeing great results! It's an active but relaxing way for both of us to loosen up. For me, it gives me time to loosen through my lower back and get onto my seat bones, find a nice tempo in the walk and maintain that tempo consistently.

It helps my horse loosen "over the top line," getting longer through the neck and back, and then shorter, in a low-impact, non-rushed pace that gives him time to adjust himself physically and mentally to each posture. All the while, he practices swinging in the walk, stepping deep underneath his body with his hind legs and also maintaining a consistent tempo.

And I get to tune in and tone up, preparing for the more active portion of the ride!

The Exercise
1. Stretch
Start on a large 20-metre circle.

Ask for a stretch, focusing on letting out your reins *as the horse reaches for the bit* and takes it out and down.

Don't just drop the reins and hope for the best. Use your seat and legs to initiate the horse's stretch, and feel for the right moment to let the reins out through your fingers.

When in stretch, feel for the swinging back. Get a friend to observe you to tell you if your horse is at least tracking up in his footsteps, or preferably over-tracking. Then also encourage your horse to open up his poll so that he reaches for the bit even when his head is at the lowest point.

2. Contract
After a few steps (let's say 5-8 steps), ask for increased impulsion using both legs. *As the horse lifts his head*, begin to shorten the reins. The horse's head and neck should lift now to his "normal" height (the height will depend on your horse's conformation and level of training) and your reins should be at your normal, working length.

Now, you want to try to maintain that swing of the back that you had in the stretch, even while the horse is contracting his top line muscles and rounder in the back and neck. You want to maintain the walk tempo that you had during the stretch. The stride length will be shorter but ideally, you want to be tracking up even in this "medium walk". The activity stays the same - no dawdling and stopping your own seat (no vacations!) just because you're walking.

Combined, I call this the "accordion" exercise, as the horse alternately stretches and contracts the back, much in an accordion fashion.

3. Now take the exercise around the ring.

Start with the 20-metre circle, but you don't have to stay there. Go to the rail and follow the rail for a few accordions, then come off the rail and change directions on a diagonal line with another accordion, the change directions and keep going.

It is important that you can stretch at will, on a line or curve, and in any place in the arena (scary locations, anyone?). Stretching when your horse wants to spook is a GREAT way to develop confidence and trust from your horse. Just be on guard and don't let the reins out if your horse is ready to run!

4. What next?

Time yourself and try this for 5-10 minutes. Stretch, contract and repeat, even if you think you're getting bored, or if you don't have your horse's undivided attention. Get you and your horse used to how it feels to let the muscles loosen, and how it feels to tighten them again after that looseness. Feel for strength in the medium walk.

Then you can do more! Why stop there? Do the same exercise in trot (more difficult) and canter (most difficult). Don't worry if things don't go perfect the first time - just keep at it and see what you need to adjust through each stretch/contract cycle.

It will get better over time. You will enjoy the fact that your horse will start to predict when he needs to come up and go down, and he will become more and more comfortable in both positions. And so will you!

Notes

Although we are thinking about the position of the head and neck, the idea is that the neck muscles are connected to the withers, which are connected to the muscular structures beneath the saddle all the way to the croup.

Stretch the neck, and you stretch the back.

But it is imperative that you also consider the hind end!

So while you are stretching, impulsion is key. With each thrust of energy, the horse reaches underneath the body, thereby creating a better balance point in terms of biomechanics, but also activating the hind end muscles into their own stretch.

You want to maintain a light but steady contact at all times through this exercise, even at the stretchiest point. Long or short reins - keep some communication going through tiny half-halts.

8. HOW TO STRETCH YOUR HORSE OVER THE TOP LINE

If you are a yoga aficionado, you might relate to thinking of the (horse) stretch over the topline as a sort of moving savasana. After completing a series of movements requiring contractions and releases (collection and extension), allow the horse to just "let go" for a few minutes, whether in walk, trot or canter, using the savasana-like stretch over the topline.

But don't just let the reins go to the buckle and become a blob on your horse's back. There is a real art to stretching the horse so that it is beneficial for him. If you just let the reins go, the horse has nothing to reach for and gets longer and longer (disengaged in the hind end), heavier and heavier (on the forehand) and hollower and hollower (over the back exactly where your weight is).

This *sort-of* stretch is not only counterproductive to the development of your horse's muscles, but also teaches him that he can't rely on you to be his partner in movement.

If you drop him, he learns to drop you.

So what's the alternative? Here are the aids to develop a functional (or effective) stretch over the top line. You can stretch at any gait assuming that the horse doesn't just speed up and run away. The stretch is most useful for encouraging the horse to release the muscles especially over the back and under the saddle.

1. Take Contact

Just be careful to not actually pull back. There is a difference between shortening the reins and feeling the horse's mouth, and pulling backwards on the rein. If you notice your elbows going further back than your torso, you are pulling too much. Just shorten the reins until you feel the pressure, and stay there.

2. Use Seat and Legs

This part is the "ask" for the stretch. Use two legs together to engage the hind end. Immediately after that, the seat initiates and encourages the stretch by scooping up and forward to the front of the saddle. You can also lighten your seat - not by tilting your body forward (as in two point), but by just becoming lighter in the saddle.

Up till now, you still have *the same level of contact* that you established in part 1.

3. Allow the Horse to Pull the Reins Out of Your Hands

This is where things get tricky. Most people want to just throw the reins forward toward the horse's mouth. If you've ever tried it yourself, you'll know how it feels when something is just let go. Instead, you should wait for a few strides.

Once your horse takes pressure on the rein, you can let the reins out a tiny bit at a time. Even now, don't just throw the reins at the horse. Have a soft, marshmallow feel to the reins and let him *take* the reins out of your hands.

4. Stretch Forward and Down

This is critical. The whole point of the stretch is to elasticize the topline. To do that, the neck must move forward (to stretch the topline muscles) and down (to reach the muscles behind the wither area). So lengthening the neck straight ahead at the normal head height does not qualify for a stretch.

Of course, lengthening the neck up to the sky isn't the answer either, because the muscles behind the withers are not stretched and probably must even contract. There should be a round arc in the neck and steady contact to make it an active stretch.

5. Take the Nose Forward and Out

The key to the stretch is for the horse to take the nose forward and out at the bottom of the stretch. It shows a softness in the poll area and ensures that the stretch occurs "from the nose to the tail". If your horse stretches forward and down but keeps his head tucked under, don't worry too much but lightly push the reins forward to encourage him to take the nose forward.

Just keep that steady contact and wait for him to learn to take the reins forward even in that position. Keep asking with your aids (#2) and calmly and steadily wait with the contact. Let the reins out at the first hint of pressure from your horse.

What if your horse doesn't take the reins?

This happens all the time, especially for horses that are not used to stretching, or for riders who are new to it. There is nothing else to do. You can't take *more* pressure, kick more, lean forward, or get agitated. The only suggestion I have is to wait. Pick up your contact, ask with your aids again (#2) and wait.

Look for any response in the right direction. If your horse even thinks about taking the reins out of your hands, lighten your fingers - but don't throw the reins forward - and patiently wait for him to take the reins from you. It will come in time.

Incorporate the stretch at the beginning of your ride to loosen up his topline and set a calm, elastic frame of mind. Use the stretch at the end of the ride to "shake out" the muscles. Use it through your ride to re-establish a soft, swinging topline.

Once your horse discovers the stretch, he might *want* it periodically through your rides. Listen carefully and use the stretch like you'd use it for yourself - all the time!

9. WALKING THE WALK IN HORSE RIDING

There's the walk, and then there's the WALK. Let me explain.

If you've ever ridden with endurance riders, you'll know what a walk really is. That's because they do it - a LOT!

I learned all about the walk when I had the good fortune of spending a week with some of the top competitive trail riders in our area (many years ago now), when I was a newbie distance rider. You'd think that the horses and riders that do 50-100 miles in a day would spend their practice rides galloping across the fields for hours on end, working harder at home so they were better prepared for competition day.

As I was about to learn from the riders that took me under their wings, nothing could be further from the truth. It was quite the opposite. While there were times during each ride that they'd go for extended trot and canter sessions, they would spend hours on end simply *walking* their horses to ultimate condition.

You can imagine my disappointment to discover that my first extended conditioning ride was going to be spent mostly at the walk. You'd probably think (as I did): walking can't possibly make that sort of athletic impact for a horse (or rider).

I think it took only that first ride for me to have a much deeper appreciation for WALKING (not just walking). As it turned out, we weren't going to go on a dilly-dallying, sauntering, swinging to the left and right kind of meandering thing. It was quite the opposite.

Lucky for me, my mare, Kayla, already had a supremely active natural walk. All I had to do was let her go, and learn to ride the gait she offered. We worked at keeping up with the others ahead of us, truly "warming" up as time passed. You know, you can break into a substantial sweat this way.

The riders taught me that the walk is physically low impact, but can play a large part in conditioning the horse - something that was key to success in long distance trail. They called it "LSD" - long, slow distance.

I learned the WALK kind of walk on the trails, but never really transferred the concept to ring riding until I began my dressage lessons years later. As I was literally re-learning all about each gait (and specifically, impulsion), I began to connect the dots when it came to walk.

In dressage, we want the walk to be active and engaged. We want the hind legs striding underneath the body. We want a "swinging" back that feels more like a trampoline and less like a rigid board. We want the horse's shoulders flowing freely and reaching straight ahead.

(Just like we did it on the trail.)

This medium walk is the foundation for the other gaits, and serves once again as a low-impact way to reach the horse's hind legs, the back, the poll - in fact, the whole top line that should release tension.

The clincher is that we are not on the trail when we're in the ring. The horse might not be as inspired to reach and engage while walking from one end of the arena to the other. This is when it becomes our job as the rider to teach the horse to move with better freedom and regularity, to march like there's somewhere to go.

In the beginning

At first, all you want is the enthusiastic forward-moving response of the horse. You might leave the reins long while you encourage a stronger, deeper stride from the hind end using your leg and seat aids. Any forward response is good and should get a quick "yes" response from you.

Your job, after you've initiated (allowed) the increased energy and movement, is to *ride it*. But be sure that you move with the horse, and resist swinging heavily on his back. Swing through your lower back but hold yourself through the core to keep your upper body as quiet as possible.

Development

Eventually, especially if you ride dressage or other disciplines that require a more compact horse outline, you will need to shorten the reins enough to keep the horse round and less strung out.

The trick at this point is to try to keep the walk as active and engaged as above. It takes a fair amount of skill and strength from the horse to maintain a free-flowing walk with a rounder, shorter body outline. But it feels amazing when the horse is "on the aids" and still moving freely through the body. Your horse will like it too.

If you do ask for this WALK consistently, it will get easier for both you and your horse. Your horse will expect to move with purpose.

If you have a sluggish or tight-moving horse, and you have access to trails, you can develop the walk in the great outdoors. Later, you can transfer it back to the riding ring.

Wishing you a happy, healthy, warming-the-body kind of WALK!

SECTION 2: LEFT AND RIGHT

10. HOW TO CHANGE DIRECTIONS IN THE RIDING RING

Well, I know that you can change directions just by turning around and going the other way! That's not exactly what I'm talking about!

There are four basic ways you can change directions in the dressage ring. The figures are designed to help you and your horse change rein without losing balance or forward energy. There are several goals for these figures:
- smooth change of direction (no cutting corners or diving)
- allow time for the horse to go straight a few strides between bends
- allow time for the inside hind leg to come deeper under the body to help in maintaining balance through the change
- allow (encouragement) for energy to be maintained

Across the Diagonal

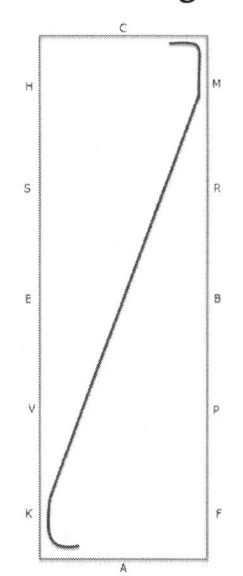

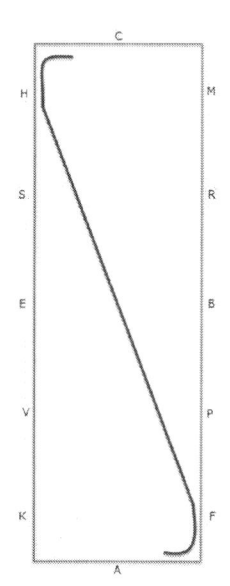

The key to the change of rein across the diagonal is to ride a good corner. Instead of cutting through the corner on an angle, go straight so that you have the 3 or 4 strides to prepare for the turn. You can do a shoulder-fore as you turn so that you are already bent slightly in the direction of the turn that's coming up.

Then ride out to the corner letter, aim straight into the diagonal line, and head off in a powerful trot through to center line. You will have plenty of time to establish flexion for the new bend, long before you get to the rail at the far end. Then go into the corner again, shoulder-fore position to set up for the new bend.

Through Center Line (E to B or B to E)

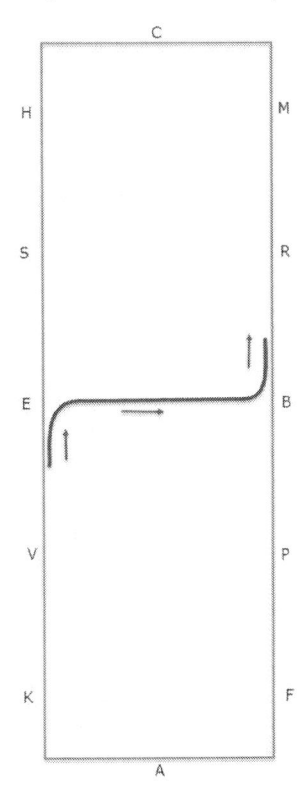

You can also change reins across center line. This line is shorter than the diagonal lines and requires a tighter turn going into and out of the line. However, the set-up is exactly the same.

According to this diagram, you'll be on the right rein coming toward E. Three or so strides before E, establish flexion and set up the shoulder-fore position. This will help your horse engage the inside hind leg, create a small bend, and position into the turn, *before* turning.

Then turn before you get to E. If you wait for E, your turn will end up drifting too far off the line, and you won't pass over X.

Straighten as you go over X, then prepare for the turn at B, exactly as you did for E.

This change of direction is more difficult simply because of the smaller space available, but it does help you and your horse learn to bend, balance and bend again.

The Tear Drop

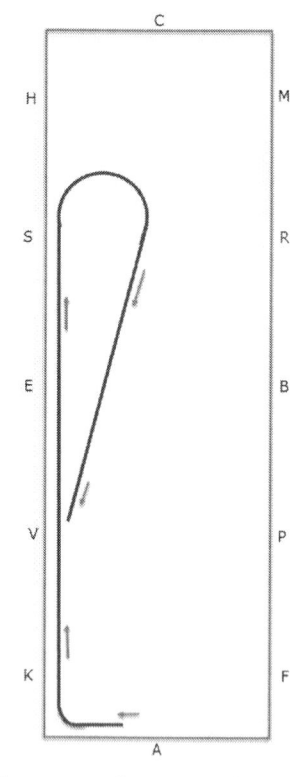

I personally love the tear drop and use it many times in a riding session. The straight line up the rail allows your horse to develop strength and momentum, and the half-circle after

S helps to contain the energy. You can do a 10 or 15-meter half circle at the top of the tear drop, depending on your level of training. Leave the rail after S and keep the circle even. You might notice that the horse has a tendency to drift on the turn, either going too far towards C or to the opposite rail.

That is the fun of the tear drop! You will learn how to use your outside rein to contain the size of the circle, as there are no walls to help you.

After the half-circle, you head back to the second letter before the corner (V in this example) on a straight diagonal line. Then navigate through the corner again, this time in the opposite direction.

Lots there to keep you and your horse attentive!

You can then go on to doing a new tear drop on the opposite rail in the new direction.

Center Line

Well this one is a given, but it's not necessarily easy to do without enough practice. The line is long! It takes even strength in the hind legs and even aids from the rider to move straight for that many strides.

The tricky part of making your center line land ON the center line is that you have to start the turn long before you get to the letter (A or C). Just like the E to B line, if you wait for the letter, you'll overshoot the line by several strides.

If you are using a regulation size ring, you might be surprised at how quickly you have to turn. It's only 10 meters from the corner to the middle letter, so you basically have to start turning as you complete the corner, and keep turning until you are on the straight line. Many riders drift on these turns and it might take some time for you to get a good feel of the size and shape of those turns.

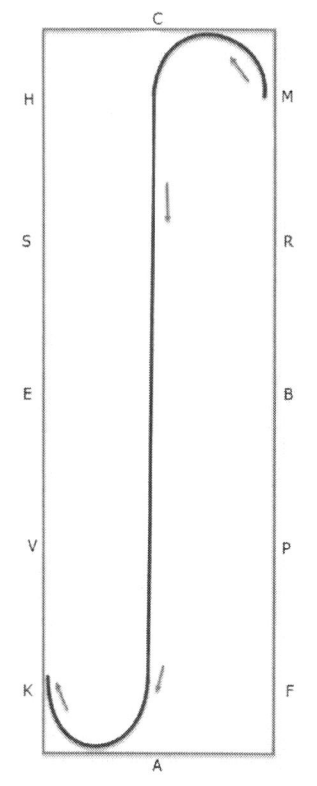

♦ ♦ ♦

Well, there you have it!

You can use these changes of directions at any gait. If you are in canter, you can do a simple change through trot or walk. Or if you're advanced, you can do a flying change at the middle point of the line. The key is to stay on the line while you change leads.

The next time you want to change directions, think of one of these figures and plan ahead to make them smooth, balanced, strong in gait, and accurate. Work those bends so that you develop your horse's lateral suppleness.

And most importantly - have fun!

11. WHAT BEND REALLY MEANS

Bend in horse riding can be explained fairly easily: the horse bends his body into the arc of the circle that he is travelling in. Think of the curve of a banana as an image in your mind.

Although it's not possible for the horse to actually bend his spine (the way you see in drawings showing a horse along an arc of a circle), the horse can bring both his hind end and his front end "in" (toward the inside of the circle). This allows him to maintain better balance as he negotiates the curve of the circle.

Sounds pretty simple, right? Then you get to work on it and discover the seemingly endless things that can go wrong.

Bend is something you can start fairly early in your riding career (or your horse's training career) but you'll notice that it's one of those things in horse riding that never really becomes perfect. Just when you think you've got it, you'll discover something new that will make it easier, softer, bouncier, looser... and you will just keep dipping deeper into that proverbial well that is "bend".

Not a bend.

Let's start with what isn't a bend.

The Neck Bend

We often think that pulling on the inside rein will get the horse bending. So we pull away, and the horse bends... his neck.

This causes the horse to send his neck into the direction of the turn, but his body doesn't necessarily follow. Instead, he now has to negotiate balance without the use of his neck (which is essential for balance). His inside hind leg is also blocked by the pressure on the inside rein, which then forces him to disengage in the hind end. This causes further balance problems.

Haunches-Out

Sometimes we can keep the front end on the arc of the circle, but leave the hind end to itself. In this scenario, the horse travels along the circle with the haunches trailing off the arc. While the front end looks like the horse might be on a bend, the awkward hind end means only one thing: *not* bend!

Flexion

Other times, rather than pulling the neck around, we ask only for the horse's head to turn in. We leave the neck straight(ish) but instead, ask for the horse to look in the direction of the turn. So while the horse's head is directed into the turn, his body may be straight or even mildly counterbent as he moves along the circle.

While flexion is a component of bend, it is not enough.

What bend really means.

A true bend is a combination of the head, the front end of the horse and the hind end. It's a whole-body position that requires suppleness throughout the body.

First, ask for flexion. The horse looks in the direction of travel.

Second, bring the front end to the turn. Use your inside leg to push the horse to the outside rein. Your leg is responsible for the control of the inside shoulder. Even though the inside shoulder must step toward the arc of the circle, make sure that the horse isn't just "falling in" - cutting the turn so that you end up coming off the circle onto a sort-of diagonal line. This is the job of the inside leg.

The outside rein (often called a neck rein) maintains the arc of the front end. Not too much arc but not too little. Just enough for the circle you're on. It also acts as the turn aid when you want to move into a turn.

Third, bring the hind end to the turn. The haunches can come in "just enough" to maintain the arc through the body. This job goes to your outside leg, which encourages the horse to bring the hind end off the straight line and into the turn. It also prompts the horse step underneath better with his inside hind leg, which will help him have better balance through the turn.

This is the overall picture.

Let's say you are travelling down the rail to the right and you have a 20-metre circle coming up at E. You move along the straight line (probably in a small shoulder-fore as you set up for the turn). Then as you pass E, you start heading into the circle.

Get the flexion even before you leave the rail - so the horse is looking into the direction of travel. Front end comes into the turn and the hind end follows, with the haunches also on the arc of the circle.

♦ ♦ ♦

At first, you might have trouble coordinating all the aids - inside leg, outside rein, outside leg. You might get one aspect of the bend but not the other two. Your horse might be stiff in the front end, the hind end or both.

Then you might get a bend but it feels like you're working really hard. Maybe there isn't enough impulsion, or the horse "leaks" in the shoulders or hips.

Eventually, though, it gets easier - for both you and your horse. You become looser, more supple. Your aids can be softer. Your horse can distribute his weight easier on the turn.

Then you develop that suppleness into all the gaits. Each gait has a different feel.

Then you learn there is even more - something called the (intentional) "counterbend" (or "renvers" in dressage). But that is a story for another day!

12. "INSIDE LEG TO OUTSIDE REIN" – THE CHEAT SHEET

How often have you heard that term? Sure, it sounds like a pretty simple concept until you try it - from coordinating your aids, to helping your horse develop an understanding... it can be more complicated than it looks.

I find it helps a lot to think of this as one whole movement, rather than breaking it down into little bits. However, to gain a true understanding, and to begin to train your body, you may need more information in order to make it all happen in one movement. So let's break it down.

Final Picture

As it can get complicated, I'm going to start with the final picture to give you an overview of what it is and looks like.

The action of "inside leg to outside rein" is meant to create and then maintain bend, without running forward or drifting out. In theory, the horse should respond to your active inside leg by *moving away* from your leg (in the rib cage area), thereby stepping out toward your outside rein.

Your outside rein can then become an actor in the movement by either limiting how far the horse can step outwards (as in stopping a leg yield from happening) or half-halting (to keep the horse from speeding up or falling to the forehand).

The horse should have a banana-like curve in the direction of the turn. (It is important though to realize that the horse's spine doesn't actually "bend" that much - the bend we feel is the result of the hind end and front end stepping into the turn). The degree of the curve is dependent on the circumference of the circle - the larger the circle, the smaller the bend. A deeper bend will happen on a 10-meter circle or smaller, but this is usually reserved for fairly educated horses (2nd level and up in dressage).

The Details

Here is a more detailed breakdown.

Rider's Torso: Turn your core toward the turn. Look in the direction of the turn (not past the turn though). The smaller the turn or circle, the more you turn in yourself.

Inside Seat Bone: Weight is on the inside seat bone. This is because you are going into your turn and want the horse to step up and under your weight.

Inside Leg: The inside leg applies pressure (from below the knee down) to the horse's side. The horse should step away from the pressure.

Outside Rein: The outside rein "fills up" when the horse steps away from the inside leg. Now, you can use the outside rein to turn the horse (apply pressure as a neck rein), or half-halt (to slow the leg speed or maintain balance) or just accept the bend with no further activity.

Outside Leg: The outside leg has a job too. It asks the hind end to also step away from pressure, *to the inside.* This means that the hind end should be the final component to the horse "wrapping around" the inside leg. The hind end can almost do a very small haunches-in to achieve that.

Inside Rein: While this rein should be fairly inactive, it will open slightly into the direction of the turn (not so much that your arm comes away from your body). It can act as a guiding rein for less experienced horses, or ideally, it will just "flutter" and not have a whole lot of pressure on it at all. It may need to come into play to maintain flexion if you have too much pressure on the outside rein, or the horse just turns his head to the outside naturally.

The Cheat Sheet

There is a way to make all the above happen fairly organically. Do this on the ground. Stand straight with your weight evenly distributed on both feet. Hold your hands like you're holding reins. This is what straight feels like.

Now, turn right as if you are going into a turn.

Start the turn from your middle, but let the rest of your body just do what it must do in order to allow the turn to happen. You'll notice that as you turn right, your inside rein will "open", your outside rein will come closer to the neck ("neck rein"), your inside leg and knee will soften and come a little forward, and your outside leg will automatically slide a little further back and tighten (to the horse's body if it were there).

Straighten again, and do it all in one motion. "Swoop" to the right. Then swoop to the left. Everything should just move along in tandem. This is what you want to achieve on the horse's back.

Common Problems

Most horse and rider combinations go through several stages of mistakes as they develop a really effective "inside leg to outside rein" feel.

The first thing that will likely happen when you turn your body in to the direction of the turn is that the horse will just lean in and "fall" to the inside of the arena. This is where your inside leg comes into play. It may take some time to teach your horse to step away, not into, your leg pressure. Don't despair if it takes several weeks or more. Your horse will get better over time.

You might shift your weight to the outside. This happens all the time! While we focus on using our inside leg, we tend to try to move the horse to the outside by throwing our body in that direction. Just catch yourself doing it, move back to the inside seat bone, and continue.

The horse will likely speed up when you first apply your inside leg. This is when an outside half-halt will be useful. Be sure to be crystal clear in explaining that pressure from your inside leg doesn't mean "go faster," but rather, "step away."

Another common problem might be that you have to learn how much pressure you need from your leg, and how much from your outside rein. In the meantime, you might end up with a horse that weaves left and right, looking like a squiggly worm! Be patient! It's so much about coordinating body parts, and it will take time for you to adjust each part as needed. Just keep trying, feel for the worm, and steady your aids.

I hope this helps you a little on your riding journey. Get out there and work that inside leg to outside rein!

13. SIX STEPS TO A WELL-BALANCED CHANGE OF DIRECTION

How often have you seen a horse and rider negotiate a change of direction, only to flatten out through the curve into a straight line, causing a sharp scramble, far misplaced from the original intended location? In mild cases, the rider hangs on adeptly, perhaps unseated but still able to negotiate the inaccurate change of direction. However, the sharp turn always runs the risk of unbalancing the horse to the point of tripping or stumbling, and the rider falling off.

How often has it happened to you? If your horse is used to leaning into a change, or dropping a shoulder or cutting corners, then this article is for you!

Changing directions smoothly can often be as challenging as achieving any well-balanced transition. Most horses are stronger on one side than the other, much like their human counterparts. Suppling the horse enough to be able to bear weight equally on both sides takes time, quality practice and a solid understanding of how the aids can assist the horse in maintaining balance while remaining loose and athletic through a turn.

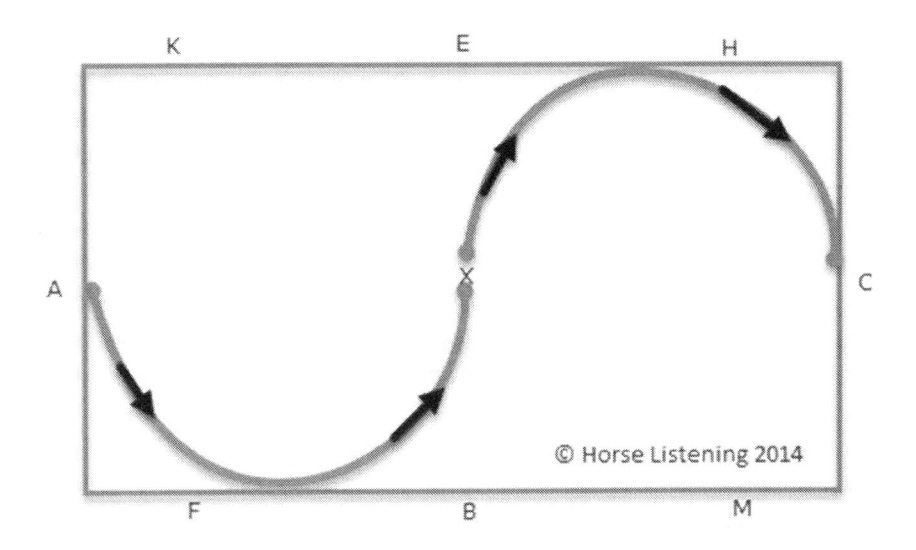

The approach to any change of direction can be narrowed down to 6 steps that are similar regardless of gait or placement of turn. Let's use this most basic change of direction as an example. I call it the "S change" (because it looks like an S and spans from one end of the arena to the other). I'm assuming you are riding in a 20x40 meter arena but please feel free to modify based on your own needs.

Let's say you are approaching a change of direction at X (in the center of the ring). You are on the left rein at A and you will go through X to turn right.

1. Approach a straight line - still bent in the original direction.

This means that you are using your left turn aids - weight on the left seat bone and body pointing slightly left. At this moment, you are riding the turn more as if it were half of a 20-meter circle, even though it won't be a full circle. You do not go into the corner of the ring. You hit the rail just past F but then come off the rail within three strides, back onto the original 20-meter circle. However, instead of continuing on the circle, you will straighten at X.

Your horse should be both flexed and bent to the left. Make sure he is looking in the direction of the turn (flexion) and also lightly bent to the left through the rib cage. Only flex and bend enough to be riding in line with the bend that is needed (in other words, don't over bend the horse).

2. Half-halt (usually on the outside rein).

Several strides before you come to X, apply a half-halt. This helps to rebalance your horse and lets him know something is going to change.

3. Straighten.

Now, instead of continuing on the original left circle, you are going to head right.

BUT - at this point, many people make a mistake. They often go directly from the left bend to the right. It's almost as if they are driving a car or a bicycle and turning the steering wheel (or handlebars) from left to right. This gives the horse no time to reposition his legs or carry his weight.

Instead of just switching your aids left to right, wait for a few strides. Straighten the horse and allow him to get his hind legs underneath him. As you go over X, be straight! If you give yourself 3-5 strides of straightness, your horse will be able to be much more balanced going into the new turn. So imagine that you should be straight two strides before X and two strides after X. You can always cut the number of strides shorter as your horse gets better at rebalancing into the new turn. But at the beginning, give him plenty of room.

4. Half-halt (usually on the outside rein).

Yep. Use another half-halt at or just past X. There is going to be another change to the new direction. Again, the half-halt helps him rebalance to the hind end and gives him a hint that something new is coming.

5. Flexion and bend to the new direction.

I like to break this part down into two quick stages. First, use your new inside aids (right) to get your horse looking to the right. This is flexion. Then, use your turn aids to bend the horse to the right. *Note: You are still moving straight over X at this point - do not actually turn yet.*

6. Turn.

Once you have your flexion and bend, simply allow the horse to complete the change of direction. The new bend should be in line with the new curve and you will proceed to hit the rail for 3 strides, then come off the rail. Don't go into the corner but head to C as if you are on a new 20-meter circle.

These six steps take a matter of seconds to complete. There isn't much time, so know what you're going to do ahead of the S, and then just do it!

I know what you're going to say. These 6 steps complicate matters far too much!

In fact, the steps *simplify* things for the horse. I know we all want to just sit there and let the horse handle everything, but when we can break things down into mini-steps, the horse almost always benefits - in a physical, mental and even emotional way. So riding actively, helping the horse navigate through the change of bend through a straight line, and re-balancing with half-halts invariably sets your horse up for more success in the long run.

Practice these steps in your changes of direction over and over again. If your horse has a habit of leaning into the turns, it might take a month or more of gentle repetition to see significant changes. But if you do stick to the plan, one day you might notice that your horse flows through direction changes as if he were just born that way!

14. WHAT IS CONTACT?

What do people mean when they speak of "contact"? The topic can be either (overly) simplified or (unnecessarily) complicated. This is another one of those horse riding questions that you'll get 25 different answers when you ask 25 different people. Between different riding styles, techniques, horses and riders, and the fairly abstract nature of the topic, you'll find many different responses to the simple question: What is contact?

There is good reason for the ambiguity. "Contact" is one of those things that can take years to develop and understand. Then, just when you think you've finally figured it out, you'll discover something new that changes your whole perspective and adds a new dimension to your level of understanding. Over the years, I've identified three stages of contact that I've learned and experienced. It is by no means *the* one conception of contact, but here is my take on it. Maybe it will help you as you go through your riding experiences.

It's Developmental

Each stage builds on the last. While we are learning, I think that all of us go through all the stages, starting with the first one as we begin our riding careers. Then, we progress to the second and then the third over time. At one point, though, it becomes more muddled than that!

The trick is that we need to go through these stages until we develop the skills to get past them. The level you are at right now isn't where you're going to be in a couple of years' time. Finding the new level takes time, practice and stepping out of your comfort zone. As always, getting educated feedback is key.

It's worth the effort though. The further along you get, the easier and quicker it will become for you to bring a horse along - even if the horse is fairly young or uneducated.

THE FIRST STAGE: "TAKE UP" THE CONTACT

Lots of times, instructors tell students to "take up the contact." What they mean is that the reins are too long at that moment, and you should shorten the reins enough to make the reins straight.

When you take up contact, you can begin to feel the horse's mouth. This will in turn help you to support your aids for such things as stops, turns, balance (through half-halts), transitions and much more. Although the hands are the last of the aids to be applied, they nevertheless help to confirm what the rest of the body is signalling to the horse.

This is the most basic form of contact. The main point of the "take up" is that the action is initiated by you and you control how much pressure you put on the bit. You are initiating a beginning form of communication. This would be used especially for beginner riders or young or uneducated horses. While you won't finish your "contact journey" at this stage, it is where you will likely begin.

During this stage, you will be learning your other aids as well. You will be working on coordinating your seat, your legs, hands and voice to mean something to the horse. You will learn to stay with the horse and not get left behind. You will also learn to become more of an active participant (rather than passive) and become comfortable with unplanned situations such as spooks, romps and just generally getting the horse to go places.

Even if you are personally at other stages of contact, you might need to come back to this stage to educate a young or inexperienced horse for the same reasons. He will learn all your basic aids and become more comfortable with your directions.

The first stage is only a beginning but it is a necessary place to start for many reasons. However, there is so much more to come!

THE SECOND STAGE: "ON THE BIT"

Eventually, "contact" begins to take on a deeper meaning. You will find out that *just* shortening the reins won't help your horse a lot. The horse will tend to feel any pressure you put on the reins, and will often either brace or tense against your pull.

We've previously talked about how pulling is not the answer to achieving healthy and quality movement. The simple reason is that every time you pull, you block the horse's energy from his hind end and through his back - resulting in a shortening of the horse's stride and a reduction in his ability to use the inside hind leg for balance.

Stage Two is when you start to notice the "pull" and do something about it. Although you know you need to shorten the reins for better communication, you begin to learn that contact cannot happen if it doesn't start in the hind end. So you begin to use your legs and seat to *initiate the shorter rein length*. Notice that the short rein happens as a result of impulsion/engagement. First, you activate the hind end. Then you shorten the reins.

When you ask the horse to engage (come under the body deeper with the hind legs), the horse's body will round more. The horse uses his topline muscles better and suddenly, your previously shortened reins seem too long! This happens because in rounding, the horse's body actually becomes shorter.

So at Stage Two, you initiate movement with your seat and legs. The horse uses that energy to round through the body and *come to* the bit. Even though you shortened the reins enough before you asked for the horse to round, it is *the horse* that takes the bit at this stage.

To repeat: *the horse* takes the bit.

You don't pull back or harder to get a result. The horse steps "forward" - to the bit. Some people call this action "seeking the bit". The only thing you do is decide on a rein length (by the way, it could be short or long - it's not the rein length that matters) and then send the horse to the bit from your seat and legs. Then you maintain balance through well-timed half-halts.

You will know this happened the first time you get it. It feels great! The "contact" is light, the horse's whole body, including the poll becomes soft, and the movement becomes bouncy bouncy - in a nice, round, trampoline-y sort of way. You will likely get a snort or two, and the horse will feel as buoyant as you do...

...even if it only lasts a few strides!

You will also feel a distinct difference between this second and the first stage of contact, when you just shortened the reins. This feel is more like you're really communicating, progressing through space together. The pull feeling is replaced by a contact feeling (if that makes sense!). You're in touch but not in a heavy way. The horse feels distinctly more powerful and round. Your aids become clearer and your horse feels freer even while he responds sooner and easier.

To recap:

Stage Two: "On the Bit"

- initiate from the hind end
- horse steps to the bit
- horse rounds
- shorten the reins
- half-halts

THE THIRD STAGE: "ON THE AIDS" OR "CONNECTION"

By the time you reach this stage, you've had lots of experience in getting the horse to move forward to the bit and developing balance both in yourself and your horse. This stage requires a good understanding and ability to do all things from the hind end (Stage Two), and more!

The next thing you need to learn is how to get the horse to "come under" in the hind end, so that he can begin to lighten the forehand. And so, we move now into "real" collection (not the just-go-slow-and-short kind).

When you first learn to collect, it feels like you have to put a whole lot of energy into it. In fact, the first time I was coming near to getting a collected trot, I felt like I was putting everything I could into the trot - and my horse's movement felt huge! But aye, here's the rub. To collect, you need more energy, deeper hind end strides (to the point that the horse starts to "bend the joints" in the hind end) and an even lighter front end.

In fact, if you do manage to get close, you might feel your horse tilt a little - and suddenly, you're sitting into a sort-of airplane-climbing-up angle. Not because you've moved your body in any way, but because the horse has. He has truly collected, and you are feeling the resultant weightlessness of the front end. Think "poll at the highest point" - not because the rider forced the horse to raise his head (and tighten his back), but because the hind end came under, the back rounded and the front end lifted.

If you can achieve this collection, even for a short period of time - because you will likely "fall" out of that balance until you both strengthen over lots of practice and time - you might feel a new type of contact that you haven't felt before.

This is what I'm terming as "Stage Three". The difference between this stage and the previous two is that the contact is incredibly light yet super "connected". It's like your horse can really read your mind, although you know it's more physical than mental. It's like you're both floating along in this togetherness that is touch, but not necessarily pressure.

I imagine that dance partners find this connection, as do pairs skaters. They are together at all times, in contact or not, but always lightly connected.

Here's the catch. This type of contact, or connection, doesn't happen from the hands. In fact, it's impossible to keep with the reins. It comes from balance. It comes from the horse's hind end. It's a position, or a posture, and it can happen because of the horse's ability to maintain that balance through his movement.

There's another catch. If you can't balance with him, you'll lose it in no time. So even if your amazing instructor can teach your horse to collect - and get the balance and connectedness - once you're on, you'll have to maintain it! Because this level of contact comes only from the kind of balance which results from your aids. Your horse can only do what you can do.

Once you get used to it, you will ride from all your aids more than from your hands - which can be termed as "on the aids". So you communicate most with your horse from your seat, your legs, your weight, even your head position - and last of all, your hands.

You can control your horse's leg stride from your seat.

You can control your horse's leg speed from your seat.

You can change your horse's gait, ask for more engagement, and encourage self-carriage and from your seat and legs.

You can turn from your entire body, which positions into the upcoming turn.

And so on.

You ride "from your aids". This is the magical space that "self-carriage" happens. Think of terms like "harmony" and "invisible aids".

To recap Stage Three:

- Hind end steps under
- Hind end tilts (engagement)
- Front end lightens (self-carriage)
- Super soft but connected "contact" - on the aids, not just on the bit

The Fluidity of the Stages

Although I've identified three stages of contact (I'm sure you can think of others or different paths to the same result), there's one more thing to keep in mind. The stages don't happen sequentially like a 1-2-3 method. They don't work like you're on a path where one stage happens, then the next and finally you arrive at the third stage.

The real-life experience is quite the opposite. The stages are there at all times, and you might fluctuate between all three, in one ride. So you might start with having to take up the contact yourself, and in a matter of minutes, achieve the level of engagement that allows you to communicate through your aids.

Then you try a new movement, and it all falls apart again and you find yourself at Stage One again. Or it happens that one day, your horse feels great - and/or you came home from an inspiring clinic and are super charged to ride - and everything works at Stage Three - just for that day!

Or, maybe you and your horse can reliably work at Stage Two - over the back and on the bit - during almost the whole ride, regardless of what the actual movements are. Other times, you can get a feel of Stage Three but then you end up at Stage Two for most movements, and Stage One when you try something new.

The Stages are fluid, interconnected but not necessarily dependent on each other.

♦ ♦ ♦

What's the point of identifying and discussing the three stages?

First, to identify the terms and create a conceptual framework around them.

Second, to give you an overview of where you are and where you might be heading.

Third, to let you know that we're all working on the three stages at one time or another, and that it's not a problem to be fluctuating between the three until you can consistently maintain yourself and your horse at the third stage. I think that's what we're always aiming for - the highest level of connection.

15. WHERE DOES YOUR HALF-HALT START? HERE ARE FOUR SUGGESTIONS

The term "half-halt" is used in the English riding disciplines, and the Western folks call it a "check". In both cases and regardless of bit type and rein length, the feeling that goes through your body is the same. Because under most circumstances, the half-halt shouldn't start from your hands.

What it's not:
- a jerk
- a strong and steady pullback
- a taking up of rein followed by a full drop of rein
- a sideways movement of the reins either left or right or both
- a turning of the wrists downward

Technically, it's not something done by the hand. Although the hand certainly plays a role in the end of the sequence of aids, it shouldn't be where the aids begin.

> *Because just messing around in the horse's mouth isn't where the riding's at!*

The Whole Body Half-Halt

Good riders ride from the body.

They use their seat, their torso, their abs, their legs. They stay tall and supple in their position, and rather than allowing the horse to carry their weight in the mouth (through a non-releasing rein aid), they influence their horse through every other aid possible. The hands become the icing on the cake after the body has done the talking.

In all the cases below, the hands strive to do nothing but stay lightly closed and steady. They *should* take up the rein so that the horse can feel some contact, but they don't use pressure to cause pain in the mouth. Instead, they work with the torso to send one collaborative message to the horse. The elbows should be on the body, softly bent and allowing or resisting as needed. The rein and the bit in the horse's mouth should be the *last part* of the aid sequence.

Let's take a closer look at where the half-halt actually originates.

1. The Seat

Most half-halts will originate at the seat. This is the area that is in direct contact with the saddle, and the root of our balance and position. By resisting the horse's movement through your seat, you will bring the horse's energy and weight more to his hind end and therefore off his forehand.

So as he goes along, you can either flow along (release) or resist (brace) to stop his forward (and maybe downward) energy. You can tighten through your legs, your thighs and "grip" more with your rear end (!!).

In any case, the horse will feel this through the saddle. His response will come from his back rather than his mouth. Beware of using too strong a seat and stifling the horse's flow of energy. You want to resist for a few strides, *in rhythm* with the horse's movement, and then harmonize.

2. The Lower Back

You can focus your attention a little higher in your back, to the lumbar area. Rather than gripping with your seat, your back does most of the resisting. In making a slight backward motion in rhythm with your horse's strides, the lower back can send a softer, less demanding half-halt.

Use this starting point for a "ballerina" horse - the one that doesn't need much input and responds quickly and honestly.

3. The Upper Back

This half-halt helps the horse lift the front end more than the others. If you begin your aid from just behind your shoulder blades, you can influence the horse's head height and the amount of weight he is putting on his front legs.

Use this starting point for the "rooters" - the horses that grab the bit and plow down to the ground. It gives you a nice alternative to just slamming the horse in the mouth with the bit. This way, he learns to actually rebalance himself rather than having to deal with pain in his mouth.

4. The Hands

Did I just say that the half-halt shouldn't start at the hands? Well, there might be one time when you can use just finger strength (although your arms are still part of your torso as you move along with your horse).

If your horse is already on your aids, and he feels soft and supple and is confidently moving along, you might want to just *not* stop your communication with him. You might want to keep the flexion of his head, or softly touch his tongue to prepare for a transition. You might want to just continue "talking" to him so that he doesn't end up tuning you out.

Use your fingers. Keep the same lightly-closed fist, but soften and tighten your fingers within that fist. Some people call it "squeezing a sponge" because that's what it should feel like. Pay close attention and see if you can literally feel the horse's tongue in your fingers.

Just remember that you can't do even this lightest of half-halts without the seat and the body. The hands must be a part of the body's communicating aids and not acting on their own.

So there you have it. I use these half-halt locations interchangeably, depending on the horse and how he feels. I find it helps to zero in on the specific body parts so that you can intentionally send the message you want to send.

SECTION 3: STRAIGHTNESS

16. STRAIGHT LINE TO TURN OFF THE RAIL (THE TEAR DROP)

The tear drop requires you to go up the rail, then turn off the rail. Let's take a moment to analyze just that movement.

First off, you are going down the rail. When you're on the rail, make sure you're *on* the rail. This means that your horse is moving in a straight line, parallel to the rail, with good energy and tempo (not too fast, not too slow but with plenty of power). Take a look at your horse's body position as you go down the rail. Is he pointing diagonally outward with his shoulders? Are his haunches further in than the shoulders? Note also your own body alignment. If your shoulders are pointing out to the rail, then you're horse's shoulders are also right there with you!

If so, then be sure to do a shoulder-fore to regain straightness in the horse's body. By bringing your horse's shoulders in toward the center of the ring - even if it's just literally a foot inward - you will help your horse straighten through the spine and travel in a true line. The shoulder-fore will also help set up your departure from the rail into the half circle of the tear drop with a mild bend and flexion.

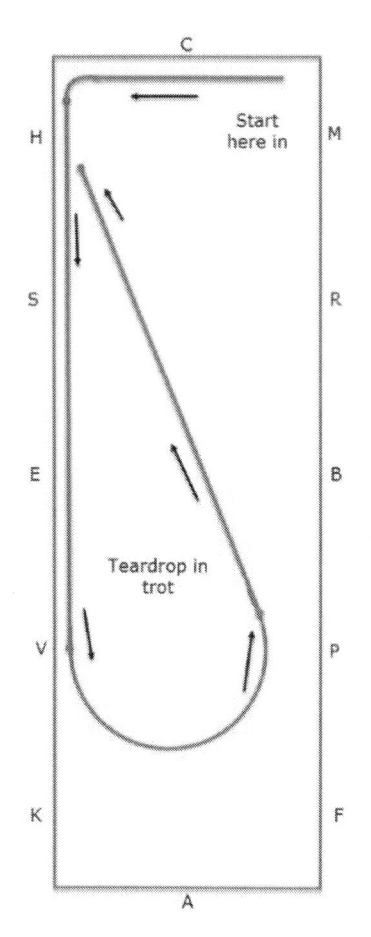

Prepare to come off the rail with a half-halt. Then leave the track.

Know where you want the horse's feet to go ahead of time. Plan about a quarter circle ahead, and take him there. Now that you're off the track, you need to keep your horse more "between your legs and hands" because there is no rail to help keep him up!

The turn can be simplified if you move your body as a whole. Try to keep as calm and quiet as you can in your body. Don't think too much about your individual hand and leg aids. Do it all together, at once, and it should all fall into place fairly organically. You can always adjust one aid if necessary as you go along.

A common error here is to actually pull on the reins to start the turn. "Steering" with your hands often causes the horse to fall off balance, scramble into the turn even while you're still cranking his head and neck around.

In contrast, keep your hands in front of the saddle and allow the horse to turn more off your seat and leg aids. Your hands should do very little in terms of turning, and only come into play if you need a half-halt if the energy forward is too strong, or a half-halt on one rein if the horse is falling in to the middle or drifting out too far to the outside. Otherwise, keep your hands (and elbows) quiet and soft and staying in front of the saddle just above the withers.

Ride the turn with your own body. Don't lean in any direction but your shoulders can be facing the direction of travel exactly with your horse's shoulders. Avoid getting left behind or falling ahead of the movement.

The final part of the tear drop is the diagonal line that takes you back to the corner you started from. Once you've completed the half-circle, straighten yourself and your horse out on the diagonal line.

Energize over the line, and prepare your horse for the corner again, this time, turning to the right (or opposite direction). One of the benefits of the tear drop is the suppling effect you get from changing reins.

Half-halt before the corner, start with a flexion right, then a bend as you head into the corner. Then half-halt again, straighten out of corner, and go straight through the short end of the arena.

You'll see the tear drop in many of my exercises simply because it really is a wonderful way to go straight, then turn, then straight, then turn again.

17. THE POWER OF STRAIGHTNESS – AND A CHECKLIST

I don't like to get too heebie-jeebie about anything to do with horses and riding, but in a way, if there's something you want to go overboard about, it's straightness.

Straightness is critical to everything that has to do with horses and riding, but really, it's mostly for the horses. Because when the horse isn't straight, he's crooked. Which generally happens all the time, and is often not recognized. If we don't recognize crookedness, how can we even begin to work on straightness?

Now, to be fair, riding truly straight is not as easy as it sounds or looks. There is so much that goes into being straight, that it's yet another one of those things that riders spend their entire lives on: achieving some success, then falling apart, then getting better, then finding new problems as they get better, and then re-establishing what they had before... it's never-ending. And the better they get, the more there is to learn.

But that's what makes achieving skills such as straightness so great! There's so much to it, until there isn't!

So how is straightness powerful?

Well, that's it, really. Being straight is being powerful.

The energy "goes through" - the power from the hind end can be transmitted all the way to the front end. Crookedness takes the power away.

The weight is evenly balanced - so every limb carries equal(ish) weight. This helps to alleviate stress on any one part of the horse's body, whether it's the shoulders, back, hips, or particular feet.

The straighter the horse, the easier it is for him to reach underneath with the hind legs, which means it's easier to begin to work on collection.

The body is in alignment, which allows the horse to maintain better balance all around. He will have an easier time with responsiveness.

The straight horse will have an easier time with rhythm and tempo. Both become more deliberate, more intentional.

And suppleness. It sounds counter-intuitive, but the odd thing about straightness is that it helps with left to right flexion and bend. And suppleness helps with straightness.

I'm sure there are at least another hundred benefits to straightness! But I think you're probably getting my point already.

Straightness Checklist

The intention of this checklist is to give you some concrete, practical points to look for when you're actually at the barn and riding. Print it off and take it with you!

Again, there's much more to be said about the topic. This is only a place to begin.

Rider's Position
- Weight is even on both seat bones
- Shoulders straight (or parallel to the horse's shoulders) - no leaning or collapsing
- Head looking in the direction of movement (through the horse's ears), chin level to the ground
- Legs evenly draped around the horse
- Tall upper body

Rider's Aids
- Inside leg to support the inside shoulder from dropping in
- Outside leg to support the horse's hips from falling out
- Inside rein slightly open for flexion as needed
- Outside neck rein or direct rein to keep the horse's outside shoulder "in the body" (no bulging or drifting)
- Seat, leg and appropriate rein (inside or outside, but usually outside) used for half-halts

Horse
- Impulsion from the hind end (use two legs for go!)
- Rib cage straight (not bulging one side or the other)
- Shoulders are aligned with the body (not bulging)
- Neck is straight (not over bent in one direction)
- Head is straight and looking in the direction of movement (no tilting, or one ear lower than the other)
- Horse is stepping straight with each step (legs do not deviate off the line)
- Horse's hind leg footsteps follow along the same line as the front leg footsteps

Well, this should be enough to get you started. Even if you can improve on one area over the next little while, it will help you along your straightness path. For example, maintain your position while the horse steps straight with each footfall. That should take a fair amount of dedication to start with!

Now there is one thing I haven't mentioned yet.

Straightness is not JUST about travelling in a straight line. So you can be straight on a circle. You can be straight on a bend. You can be straight in a movement, like leg yield or walk pirouette. You can even be straight on a half-pass, even while the horse is bent in the direction of movement while travelling diagonally across the ring.

This is because straightness is about the alignment of the horse's (and rider's) body. So even while the horse is bent into a direction, he has to maintain "straight" alignment through the hips, ribs, shoulder, neck and head. If he isn't straight, then he'll have a bulging shoulder, or rib cage, or hips swinging out.

And now you can see how straightness permeates pretty much everything we do while riding, from the beginning levels all the way up. And the secret is that it's not always necessary to work on trying to straighten single parts of the horse's body. In fact, you want to develop the other qualities of movement: rhythm (and tempo), suppleness, connection (and contact), impulsion... all of the basics that are discussed in the dressage Pyramid of Training. The better you get at the basics, the quicker and easier it will be for the horse to move correctly, and eventually, straight.

18. WHAT IS A NECK BEND? AND WHAT TO DO ABOUT IT

Have you seen a horse doing the neck bend? Maybe you do it unintentionally, thinking that it "feels right".

On a turn, you "bend' the horse, and the horse's neck comes far to the inside. The body continues on the same original arc, but you've got that head and neck pointing in the direction you want to go!

Sometimes, the horse's body actually drifts out even though the neck is pointing in. Other times, the horse takes a tight turn to the inside, almost stumbling over his front legs because of the sudden movement.

Neck Bend

The neck bend looks exactly as it sounds. The rider goes to bend the horse, and instead of achieving a tail-to-head arc through the body, only the neck juts to the inside. It looks almost like the neck comes off the body and does its own thing, regardless of what the rest of the horse is doing.

It might be caused by the rider who is pulling the neck in with the inside rein, or it might be caused by the overly one-sided horse who prefers to carry his neck to one side of the body. If you feel carefully, you might notice the outside rein getting longer and the inside hand pulling farther back.

The neck bend causes the horse to be imbalanced. No matter which movement he performs, his neck is essentially taken out of the equation and the horse moves out of straightness. Crookedness can cause many problems over the long-term, from misbehavior to soundness concerns.

Needless to say, all horses and riders have a stiffer and a more supple side. We work diligently on developing both sides equally in effort to become truly ambidextrous in the long run.

From Neck Bend to True Bend

Straighten the neck. I know this sounds counter-intuitive. You want to bend so the neck should be bent, right? Well, not exactly. Make sure that the neck comes out of the shoulders naturally. Use your outside rein to support the neck and shoulders. If the horse wants to take his neck to the inside, use a resisting (not pulling backward) neck rein to prevent him from pulling in.

In contrast, if you find yourself pulling his neck in with your inside rein, stop! Even out your reins and start working on a nice neck rein to do the talking.

Let's say the horse (or you) over bends the neck to the right (this is very common).

Travelling Right
- Use very little inside (right) leg and rein
- Use a strong and steady outside (left) leg and rein

- Make sure you are not over bending your own torso and shoulders with the horse. Keep only the appropriate bend position in your body.

Travelling Left
- Use a strong and steady inside (left AGAIN!) leg and rein
- Start with a light outside leg and rein, and adjust as needed
- Work on sending the horse out to the right rein and leg, form the inside aids
- Keep an appropriate bend and position in your body.

What Does This Mean?

You will probably need to overuse your left aids (seat, legs and rein) NO MATTER WHICH DIRECTION THE HORSE IS MOVING.

Start with a mild bend and work toward a deeper bend over time.

Developing a true bend on a 20-meter circle is hard enough for a stiff horse and rider. So start there, and work on achieving and then maintaining the bend over the whole circle. As you both get stronger and more evenly supple, make the circle smaller in increments. 15-meter and 10-meter circles require progressively deeper bends. In all cases, make sure it's not just your horse's neck that is coming in but that there is a nice arc through the whole body.

It takes years for both the horse and rider to become truly supple on both sides. Every time you add a new movement, you will likely need to revisit the bend within that movement. But don't despair – just keep working on it at all times and be aware of that dreaded neck bend!

Consider this.

One note about the neck bend. In general, when you get into the habit of riding with a neck bend, it might feel *very* awkward for you and your horse to move with a straighter neck. You might feel like the horse is stiffer or even bent to the outside at times, while all you've done is brought the neck and shoulders into straightness.

But be diligent!

If your horse is used to over bending the neck to the right, you will always need that stronger left leg and rein. Even when you're going right.

While we are often taught to keep the inside rein light (I write about this all the time), don't feel like you can't change things up to correct a crookedness.

Ride the horse that you have. Always!

FOCUS ON TRANSITIONS

I. THE FIVE STAGES OF A TRANSITION

We can all use work on our transitions. Even the most educated horse and rider can always develop better transitions. There are so many things to work on if you stop to really think about the different stages that horses and riders go through as they become more secure in their aids.

Whether you are working on upward transitions or downward, progressive or non-progressive, there are certain aspects to look for in every well executed gait change.

With young horses, you'll reward even a successful effort. Once your horse has developed enough strength and balance, you can have higher expectations. Some horse/rider combinations can go through the first three or four stages over the course of a few months. Others can take longer - it all depends on each partner. Irrespective of the time it might take to go through these stages, it's good to be aware of how transitions can progress from the basic to the more advanced.

Let's start at the beginning.

Gait Change

The first goal we have for young or untrained horses is to get the transition in the first place. At this stage, we should be working mostly on communicating that the horse's legs need to change gait when we ask for it. So if your horse does change gait, you let him know he's on the right track.

You don't really concern yourself with any bobbles or hiccups along the way. If he falls to the forehand or sideways, you accept it and help him rebalance a few strides after the transition. If he rushes into the next gait, you ride the rush and do your best to harmonize. If he throws his head up or down, you allow it as long as it isn't dangerous. He is putting effort into doing what you want and you don't want to stifle his attempts in any way.

You are only developing a method of communication at this point. Encourage him when your horse begins to understand.

Throughness

The next thing to work toward is how well your horse allows his (and your) energy to "come through" during the transition. So this is when fluidity becomes more of a factor. If you put energy in (through seat and legs), it should be transferred through the horse so that he can not only change his legs to the new gait, but also allow his hind legs to step deeper underneath his body, and his top line to round even just a little.

By allowing his energy through, the horse can begin to become more supple and less tense. At this point, doing the transition can improve all of his gaits, especially because he is becoming more "ahead of the leg" (which just means that he is able to allow his energy in the front end as in the hind end).

Make sure that you are ready for an energy surge. If your horse truly "amps up" his energy, you need to ride it, not get left behind. Go with him and teach him that it's good to reach forward, especially going into and out of a transition.

Balance

At this point, you can become more careful about your horse maintaining balance before and after the transition. In my opinion, doing this sooner in his education might cause him to become reluctant to go forward. So first make sure he is willing and confident in making the transition in the first place.

A good transition is done from the hind end. So now you can ask your horse to balance just a bit to the hind end before and after heading into the new gait. This is when effective half-halts become critical.

You can prepare for a transition with two or three half-halts (in rhythm with your horse's strides), do the transition, and then half-halt again once or twice to help the horse from falling to the forehand. So basically, you are asking for balance before the legs change and then balance again after the legs are in the new gait. As your horse becomes stronger, your balancing requests can become shorter and lighter, but you may need to be "there" for your horse in the beginning.

Precision

Once you have a forward, through and balanced transition, you can start to become really picky - and expect it to happen in a specific place. So let's say you are on the rail and you decide the transition should happen in the corner before A (this is an easy way to start with a young or inexperienced horse). So give yourself three to five strides to get the transition, while you ride through that corner.

Another time, try it coming out of a corner. So you pass A and give yourself three to five strides for the transition. Try to prevent your horse from falling in off the rail at this point - you just want a leg change without a deke or a dive or a fall to the forehand.

As your horse becomes more proficient, you can start asking at a letter. For example, pick the letter A and make your transition as your leg and shoulder passes the letter. Prepare ahead of time and then ask as you go by. Then pick another letter further down the rail for another transition. Turn it into a game and see how accurate you both can become.

Finally

This last stage is really just the icing on the cake. Once you have precision, you can really get down to working on becoming invisible. It's all well and good to be able to be effective, but you can't stop there. If you haven't already developed super quiet aids in the process, now is the time to learn to "whisper". By now, your horse is on your aids, willing and confident, round and balanced, and working with you on a moment's notice.

There really should be very little that onlookers can observe. No pulling, no loss of balance, no flailing legs, no falling of the upper body, no boisterous voice command - nothing. If they watch you ride, they see *nothing* - except, of course, that the horse made the transition beautifully, seemingly on his own accord. Just plain, simple harmony.

Well, that is what we're all aiming for anyway. I do know it can be done, but I also know it might take some of us years to accomplish consistent, accurate, soft transitions. But isn't this why we're in it for the long haul? There is always something more to learn and another goal to reach.

What stage are you and your horse at in your transitions?

II. WEEK 1

Active, balanced transitions are among the most fundamental parts of riding. Transitions are like a pass in hockey, a volley to your teammate in volleyball, or the skate-up to a jump in figure skating. Without a good transition, the horse will be unable to balance into the next movement, no matter how hard he scrambles after the fact.

On week one of our Focus on Transitions, we're going to focus on walk/trot/walk transitions as well as left/right changes of direction.

I'll go over the aids for both the up and down transitions and then you'll get our exercise of the week. We'll also go through the three types of transitions. All three types can be included in our exercise.

Purpose:

Walk-Trot-Walk Transition, Change of Direction and Change of Circle Size (Bend)

Due to the 10m circle, this exercise is suitable for horses and riders with some previous training. You can simplify it for young horses or beginner riders by working on 20m circles only.

Goals:
- Balance
- Impulsion
- Beginning of topline use
- Beginning lateral suppleness
- Maintenance of rhythm through the changes
- Accuracy of circle size, 20m and 10m

The walk-trot-walk transition is a basic movement but don't be fooled by its simplicity! Many horses, trained or not, have difficulty managing a balanced, energetic transition in these gaits. We will work on the preparation to each transition to help develop impulsion to, through and after each gait change.

Change of direction and circle size is also added in this exercise to help the horse (and rider) develop a beginning level of suppleness and balance.

Aids:
Please note that these are general aids that do not necessarily resolve specific problems.

Trot Transition From The Walk

> *Start with a good walk.*
> *Prepare to trot.*
> *Trot.*
> *Go!*
> *Half-halt.*

As in, don't just drag your horse into the trot. Get a good march at the walk, preferably on a large circle with a mild bend. Establish a strong walk rhythm before heading into a trot.

Prepare to trot.

Use a mild half-halt two or three strides before the transition. Keep the strong, forward walk footfalls right to the transition (as in, don't allow the horse to slow down or conversely, speed up the last couple of strides).

Trot.

Start with your seat. Trot in your seat bones.

Add legs - even pressure on both sides. Use as little as you need, but as much as you need.

Maintain your rein length.

Don't get left behind when the horse trots off. Do you best to *not pull back* on the reins through the transition (we all do this even subconsciously). However, also do your best to *not let the reins out* during the transition. We also do this when we're trying to not pull!

Go!

After the legs change, ask for a couple of steps of increased impulsion. This might sound counter-intuitive until you realize that the horse should have increased energy to allow the hind legs to come deeper underneath the body just as the trot is beginning. Let the horse give you this slight energy surge and ride it through. Don't block with your hands through this moment.

Half-halt.
This is like the icing on the cake. In order to help your horse maintain balance through the gait change, you still need to "recycle" the energy back to the hind end. Some horses need very slight half-halts (maybe even just from a little finger squeezing on the reins) while others need a true rebalancing from the seat. You might even have to adjust your half-halt strength in different times for the same horse. Again, stick to the same rule - use as little strength as you need but as much as you need.

Walk Transition From The Trot

> *Start with a good trot.*
> *Prepare to walk.*
> *Walk.*
> *Go!*
> *Half-halt.*

You might be noticing a pattern in the transition aids.

The down transition aids are pretty much the same as the up transition aids. I won't repeat everything I already said above for the walk/ trot transition, but all the explanations would be the same - just with opposite gaits.

Use your seat the same way (switch from trot to walk), use your half-halts in the same way, and use the Step #4 "Go" the same way, after your horse is walking. Do use your leg aids as you prepare to walk. Keep your legs on in the transition.

What you shouldn't do is use your reins to pull your way into the walk. Half-halts should do nicely and then your seat can take over from there.

Exercise:
We'll start with a variation on regular figure eights.

This first diagram is drawn on a large 20x60 metre ring. The second diagram is drawn for a smaller, 20x40m ring. Unless you're using these exercises for show preparation, the size of your ring doesn't matter as much as the accuracy and consistency in size of your circles.

Let's say you are starting the exercise at C, going left.

Start with a 20-m circle to the left, at the trot.

You will go around the circle one and a half times. So, you start at C but finish on the opposite end of the circle at #1.

Transition to the next circle to the right. The catch here is that the right circle is going to be half the size of the left circle: only 10m.

Go around that circle one and a half times to #2.

Transition to the next 20m circle, going left again until you get to #3.

Finish with a 10m circle going right.

At the end of the pattern, continue on the rail going in the same direction as the last circle (right). This will take you back to C, going to the right.

Horse Listening

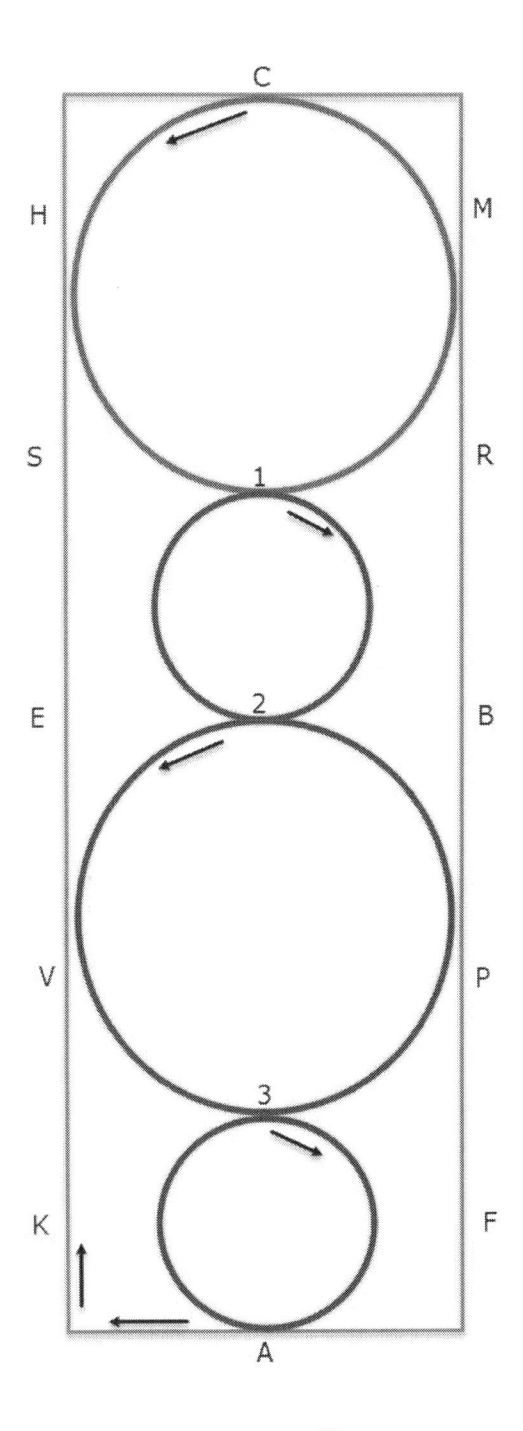

111

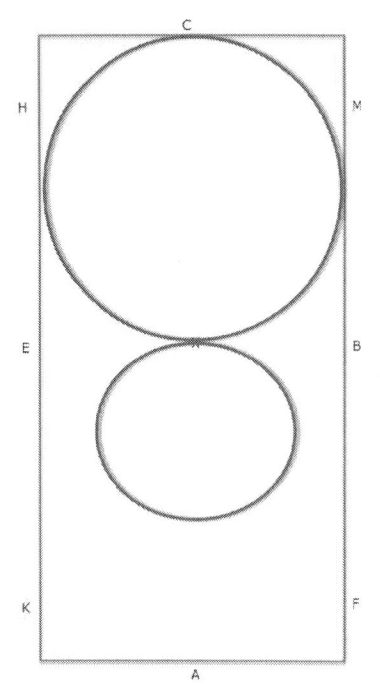

You can run through the pattern 4 times to practice each side twice.

If you're using the smaller ring pattern, you can go around each circle only once. If you use X as the midpoint between both circles, you can switch directions and circle size each time you complete a circle. This ends up being a figure 8 with different sized circles.

Transitions

There are three types of transitions in this pattern.

Each circle requires a change of direction. The repeated left and right changes will help to supple your horse laterally. Remember to use your inside seat and leg aid in preparation of the new direction.

The change in circle size helps your horse bend more on the smaller circle, thus requiring a deeper stride from the inside hind leg. Then the next large circle allows the horse to use that increased engagement into a more forward, powerful stride using a smaller bend. See if you can develop a steady tempo in both the large and small circles.

Once you have a good handle on the figure, **add gait changes within the circles**. Start at the trot and do a walk transition at each midpoint of the circle. You can make it easier for your horse by walking 5 strides. Or you can increase the level of difficulty by limiting the walk to only 3 strides. Just make sure that you do get a walk, and that the walk is at a good marching pace. Then go back to the trot.

Try this exercise a few times this week and see what you think. Does it help your horse develop better suppleness left and right? Do the 10m circles encourage your horse to lighten the front end a bit? Do you run into any problems through any of the transitions?

III. WEEK 2

Last week, we started with three forms of transitions: change of direction (bend), change of gait (walk-trot-walk) and change of circle size (20m and 10m circles). The idea was to negotiate those changes as smoothly and balanced as possible through the circle exercise.

This week, we're going to work on straight lines moving to a circle back to a straight line. In general, straight lines are even harder to do well than bends because true straightness means being equally balanced on both the left and right sides. Both horse and rider must become straight even on turn lines or bends, but on a straight line, lack of straightness is easily evident.

Purpose:

Walk-Trot-Canter-Trot-Walk Transition, Straight Line to 15-m Circle, Counter Canter

Although we are still working on progressive transitions (up and down transitions that occur in order of gaits), this exercise is somewhat more challenging than Week One. You can accommodate for young/untrained horses or beginner riders as indicated at the bottom.

Goals:
- Balance
- Impulsion
- Straight line to bend or circle
- Corners
- Accuracy of 15-m circle
- Maintenance of rhythm through all changes

Aids:

This time, we are going to transition between all three gaits, upward and downward. See the specific aids for a walk to trot and trot to walk transition in last week's chapter.

Trot-Canter Aids

Please refer to Chapter IX of this Transitions Section, 7 *Essential Aids for An Epic Canter Transition.* I feel there is sufficient detail in that description to give you a good idea for the upward transition.

Canter-Trot Aids

The aids for this downward transition are similar to the upward transition aids.

1. Seat

Your seat should be in canter mode at this time. However, you can use a resisting seat aid in tandem with your upcoming half-halts to prepare for the downward transition.

2. Half-Halt

This half-halt can start with the seat and be followed up with the hands if necessary. Use your leg aids at this moment to help keep your horse's energy flowing forward even through the downward change of gait.

3. Trot

Now, your seat should be in trot. If your horse "drops" heavily into the downward transition, be sure to use your leg aids to urge him to press on in trot. Ideally, his first few trot steps should be strong and energetic.

You should also be there right on top of him, ready to move boldly forward into the trot. Don't get left behind or jolted out of your saddle. You can go into a posting trot or continue sitting if you are able.

4. Hands

We are often taught to pull the horse into the down-ward transition, especially as new riders. Once you can reliably get the change of gait, start to work away from pulling at all for a downward transition.

The half-halts should be adequate to prepare your horse for the transition, and then to establish the trot. See if you can maintain an even pressure with your reins. Avoid both extremes - throwing them away or pulling back.

Exercise:

This exercise can be done in a large or small ring. It is drawn here using the letters of the large ring for easier reference. Start on the right rein at E, at a good, strong, marching walk.

Transition at S to trot.

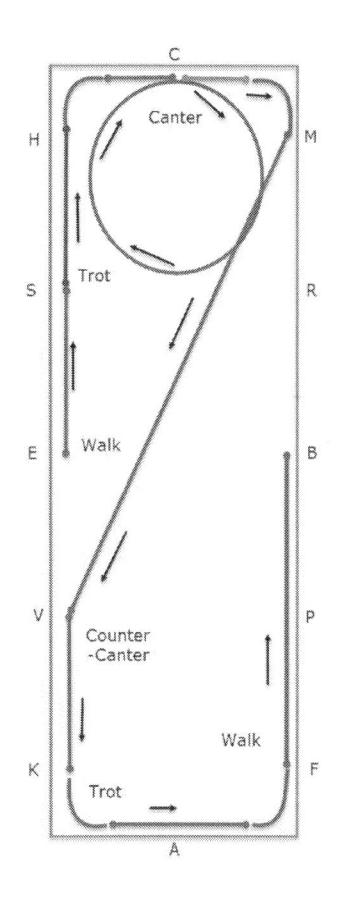

Do a "good" corner before heading to C, still in trot. Transition at C to canter. Do a 15-metre circle. Be sure to stay off the rail through the whole circle. Use your outside aids to guide the horse on the circle.

Continue to the corner, still in canter.

Complete the corner and head on a diagonal line from M to V, still in right lead canter.

Continue in right lead canter from V to K. This requires the horse to maintain a counter canter for a few strides just before the trot transition.

Trot at K. Head into the corner at trot.

Finish the second corner and transition to walk. Finish the exercise in walk to B.

Now, if you like, you can continue the same exercise on the opposite rein starting at B. If not, go back and do it again from E.

If you have a young or untrained horse, or a beginner rider, you can make a few changes that will help them be successful. Take the transition in the corners instead of at the letters on the rails. The corners help the horse maintain balance better. You can make the circle a 20-metre circle, which will help the horse that needs more room. You can also trot the diagonal line rather than negotiate it in canter/counter-canter.

Try this exercise a few times this week.

IV. WEEK 3

Purpose:
Things are getting a little more complicated this week! We're going to head into a bit more challenge with non-progressive transitions, specifically walk to canter to walk) and a walk/canter straight line transition. In general, straight line transitions are more difficult than transitions on turns (the horses want to fell left or right). There is also a canter loop and 15-metre circles at each end of the ring.

If you have a young horse or beginner rider, feel free to change the gaits to the ability level that is needed. For example, trot instead of canter, come off the pattern when needed (nothing is written is stone!) or make the circles larger. Always suit the exercise to the student and horse, and set them up for success before moving on.

Here we go!

Goals:
- Properly placed 15-metre circles
- Straight and balanced canter-walk transitions

- Effective corners
- Transitions within a straight line
- Impulsion to, through and after the transitions
- Effective half-halts before and after changes (gait and bend)

Aids:
Walk-Canter-Walk

1. Walk

Start with a strong, marching walk. Keep reins short enough for the upcoming canter transition. Legs should be on and seat is walking.

2. Prepare

Half-halt two to three strides before the canter transition. This half-halt might be just a "whispering" half-halt because you are at the walk and there is little impulsion. Be sure your half-halt doesn't block the horse, but rather, softens him over the top line and prepares him for a deeper hind end stride as you head into the canter.

3. Canter Transition

Inside leg stays firm at the girth, helping the horse stay straight.

Outside leg does a "windshield wiper" movement behind the girth.

Seat canters.

Ideally, these aids happen in quick succession, almost at the same time. Be sure that your seat continues in the canter after the first canter stride. You might need to keep your outside leg back over the first few strides to secure the canter lead.

4. Walk Transition

After achieving a rhythmical, strong canter, prepare to walk with a series of half-halts.

Both legs become active - they put pressure on the girth, asking the hind end to come underneath for the transition.

Half-halt a few strides before the transition.

Seat changes to walk.

You might need a few half-halts after the walk transition as well, to establish an active rhythm.

Exercise:

Once again, adapt this exercise to your ring size. The letters are there for reference only.

Start at the arrow, just before C. You are walking on the left rein.

Canter transition at C. Left 15-metre circle beginning and ending at C. Walk transition after C, before the corner. Walk through the corner, while preparing for another canter transition.

Canter loop from H to X to K. This requires the horse to do a mild counter-canter but maintain the left lead. You might need to encourage more activity through this part in order to maintain balance and roundness (work over the topline).

Before K, prepare to walk. Walk at K, before the corner. Walk to A.

Before A, prepare to trot.

At A, do a 15-metre left circle at trot. Continue through the corner, preparing to walk.

Walk at F. Between F and P, prepare for a walk to canter transition. Shorten the walk strides and increase the energy level. You might need to work at keeping your horse straight through this short walk as well.

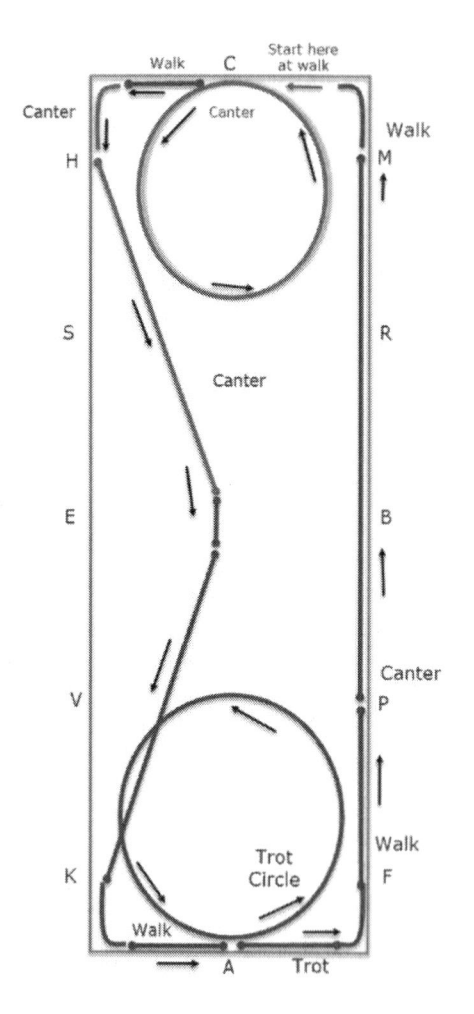

Left lead canter at P. Maintain the straight line to M.

Before M, prepare to walk. Walk at M.

You can start the whole thing over and do the left side a few times before you change directions to the right side.

I rode this exercise myself this week with Cyrus. The transitions do come up quickly and the relative "straightness" of the whole thing gives little room for rest. But it kept us on our toes and had Cyrus working well from the hind end when all was said and done! His gaits got freer and more balanced as we went through it several times. His rhythm slowed a bit and felt more purposeful at all the gaits. The walk breaks gave us a chance to gather ourselves for the next part of the exercise.

V. WEEK 4

I've saved the most interesting exercise for last! Enjoy!

Purpose:

This week, we're going to progress into more changes - including changes of bend as well as gaits. We have embedded circles at different gaits, which will require your horse to step deeper under the body and bend more than in previous exercises. We continue with straight line transitions and non-progressive as well as progressive transitions.

You can simplify the exercise by keeping to one gait for both circles. You can make the exercise more difficult by cantering the 10-metre circle and trotting the 20-metre circle.

Goals:

- Accurate 20-metre circle which transitions to a 10-metre circle
- Straight and balanced canter-walk and walk-canter transitions
- Effective use of corners at trot
- Adequate bend for 20-metre vs. 10-metre circles
- Trot to halt transition on a straight line

Aids:
See the previous chapters for the walk-canter and canter-walk, as well as the walk-trot and trot-walk transitions.

Trot-Halt Transition
This is a non-progressive, downward transition that requires more energy and response from the horse than you might think.

1. Trot
As this is the last "movement" of the exercise, you come to the halt from the 20-metre trot circle. Make sure you have a strong, round trot as you come out of the circle. If your horse has a tendency to slow down on a circle, you might need to energize him from the hind end before heading onto the straight line. If your horse tends to rush, use a half-halt or two to help him balance more to the hind end before the straight line.

2. Straight Line
You come out of a mild 20-metre bend to the rail. Be sure to keep your horse's shoulders from "leaking to the outside" and pointing to the rail. Keep the horse straight on the straight line. Half-halt through the last two or three strides in preparation for the halt.

3. Halt
Stop with your seat. Keep your legs on the horse's side, but not active. Keep contact with the reins, but avoid pulling back. Try to get the halt more from your seat than your hands. Ideally, your horse should stop straight (not leaning to one side) and square (front legs parallel and hind legs parallel).

Exercise:

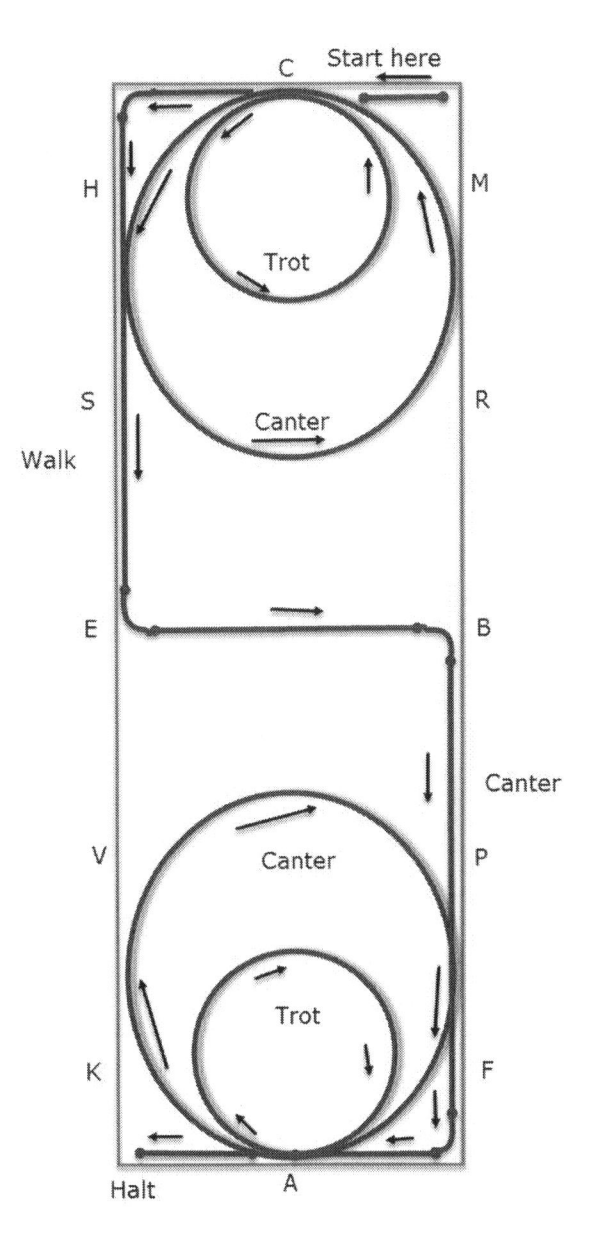

Start at Walk before C, on the left rein.

Transition to canter at C, left lead. 20-metre canter circle.

Transition to trot at C. 10-metre trot circle.

Make sure you increase your horse's bend for this circle. He might want to slow down a bit - you can accept that if you feel that the initial trot was too fast, but make sure you keep his energy up and the stride length long.

Continue at trot through the corner.

Walk at S.

Walk the sharp left turn at E, straight over X, and walk the sharp right turn at B.

Canter transition at P.

20-metre canter circle, right lead, starting at A.

10-metre trot circle at A.

Come out of the trot circle and halt before the corner.

You can walk out of the exercise and start the whole thing over again by walking across the diagonal (maybe in a nice stretchy walk?) and starting again before C. Or you can continue straight along the rail, and start at C going in the opposite direction. Your walk lines will be on the opposite sides of the rails.

Using embedded circles like this helps both you and your horse develop a really good sense of the bend and engagement it takes to transition between small and large circles. Add the gait transitions, and it's not as easy as it looks!

Happy riding!

VI. THE SIMPLE (?) HALT TO WALK TRANSITION

Just a simple halt to walk transition. We do it all the time! So what's the fuss?

In my experience, horses do something *other* than walk straight forward out of the halt. Try the transition a few times and pay close attention to what happens after you ask for the walk.

Let's break it down.

The Halt

First, develop a strong, marching walk that shows activity. In other words, the walk should be brisk and fairly up-tempo. Not so fast that it feels like your horse will break stride into trot any second; but develop a forward, reaching, free-flowing walk.

You'll know it's a good walk when the foot-falls are evenly spaced apart - 1..2..3..4. If it's more like 1..2..3.....4, then you know that it's still not a "pure" walk, or one that is rhythmical, balanced and strong.

You can prepare to halt after you get that walk!

The aid for the halt is mainly in your seat. While in the walk, you're walking with your seat bones, in rhythm with the horse's movement. Prepare to halt with a half-halt. When you halt, you stop the seat. If the horse continues to walk, don't be as free-flowing with the seat bones. Follow up with half-halts on the reins (not a steady pull) until you get the legs to stop.

Stay in halt for five seconds to really establish immobility. Work on keeping your horse's attention - no looking around!

Consider the halt as a movement rather than a stop everything. Stay toned, "connected," tuned into each other, and just wait.

But don't wait too long! If you managed the five seconds, and your horse is still with you, walk out of the halt. It takes practice to stay immobile while ready to go at a moment's notice.

The Walk

What happens during the very first step out of the halt?

Does your horse lift his head and stick the nose to the sky?

Does he take a large step left or right?

Does he take a few tiny, slow steps before establishing his normal pace?

Does he go to take a few steps backward before he realizes you wanted forward steps?

Practice

While it seems too simple, achieving a bold, powerful but contained, smooth walk out of the halt is something that must be learned by both the horse and rider. A good transition doesn't always come naturally.

Here are a few things to keep in mind as your horse takes that first walk step.

Is he ready to step out with an active hind end? One of the first things to notice is whether the horse pulls himself forward from the front end or pushes from the hind end. Make sure you are asking his hind end to move forward first. The horse should ideally step forward promptly and energetically from your two light leg aids.

Is he straight? You can notice straightness by observing his front shoulders. Do they aim straight forward, or do they step slightly sideways? Does the hind end swing to one side or the other? Be sure to keep your reins even, your legs even, and your seat and upper body pointed forward. When the horse takes the first step, make sure *you* are not leaning or weighting one seat bone over another. Urge him to go straight from your straight body and aids. Use leg aids to counter any hind end swings.

Does the horse throw the head up in those first few steps? We call this a "giraffe neck" - the head goes high, the horse flings the nose up in the air. If you try it yourself, you'll feel the discomfort through the back of your neck and shoulder blades almost immediately. When the head goes up like that, the base of the neck actually drops. The back hollows and the horse's underline lengthens.

This puts him on the forehand immediately and he has to carry your weight with a compromised balance. In this case, make sure you are not letting your reins out through your fingers, or doing the Jelly Elbows routine (look this up in the blog for more info) as you transition to walk. Find a comfortable rein length for the horse, and keep that rein length right through the transition. Keep your elbows on your body and expect the horse to walk even while he stays round and on the bit.

Intersperse the halt to walk transition through your ride as a breathing break. Just after you've done some canter and trot work, go to the walk, halt (five seconds) and walk again. It might take some practice to get the immobility and then the energy and regular footfalls of the walk after the halt.

Use it also as a cool down at the end of the ride. Before you get off, do a few halt to walk transitions.

VII. A TRANSITION EXERCISE TO JAZZ UP YOUR RIDING ROUTINE

Transitions!

Without them, where would we be?

Well, we'd be trotting the same direction ad infinitum. Cantering until both horse and rider are so out of breath that they have to stop. Posting in a repetitive motion that goes forever more... sure to develop ring sourness and boredom.

Enter transitions!

Maybe that's why I'm crazy about transitions! They're all about change. They make the ride fun, challenging, and fresh. They develop both the horse and rider's balance, coordination, sense of space and communication.

Try this "simple" (but not necessarily "easy") transition exercise just to add a little pizzazz to your normal riding routine.

It's all straight lines. Straight lines are actually not easy to maintain, and changing gait within a straight line is even harder. But it's a great way to check your accuracy!

Transitions Exercise Part 1

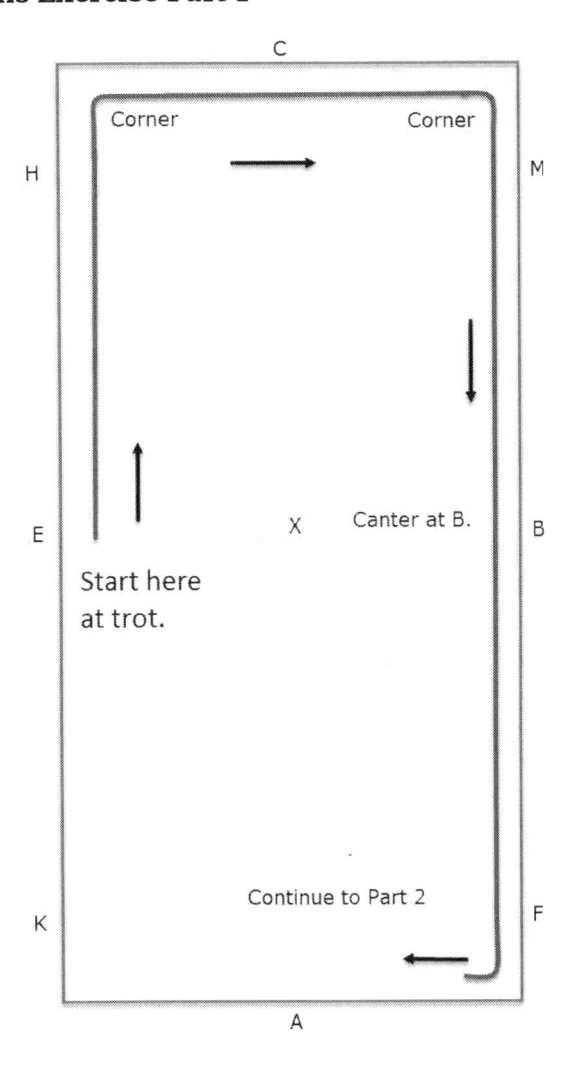

```
                    C
        ┌─────────────────────┐
        │  Corner      Corner │
      H │      ──→            │ M
        │                     │
        │                     │
        │                     │
        │                     │ ↓
        │                     │
        │   ↑                 │
      E │   │    X  Canter at B. │ B
        │                     │
        │  Start here         │
        │  at trot.           │
        │                     │
        │                     │
        │                     │
        │       Continue to Part 2 │
      K │                     │ F
        │              ←──────│
        └─────────────────────┘
                    A
```

133

Transitions Exercise Part 2

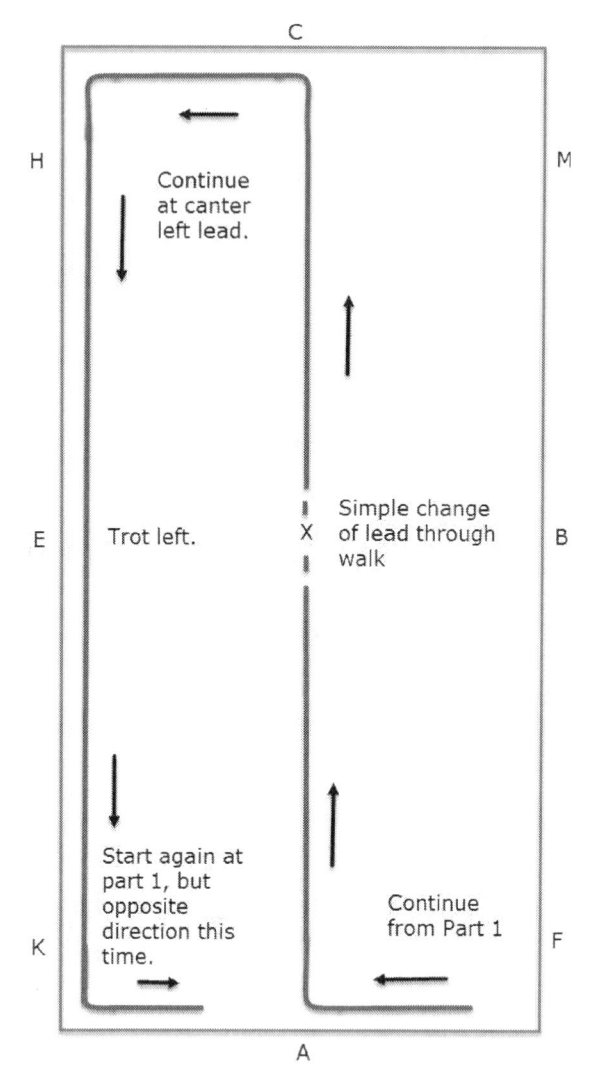

```
            C
    ┌───────────────────┐
    │       ←           │
H   │                   │   M
    │  Continue         │
    │  at canter        │
    │  left lead.       │
    │        ↓          │
    │                   │
    │             ↑     │
    │                   │
    │          ┆ Simple change
E   │  Trot left.  X ┆ of lead through   B
    │          ┆ walk
    │                   │
    │                   │
    │        ↓          │
    │             ↑     │
    │  Start again at   │
    │  part 1, but      │
    │  opposite         │  Continue
    │  direction this   │  from Part 1
K   │  time.            │   F
    │       →      ←    │
    └───────────────────┘
            A
```

In Part 1, you are riding on the rail to the right in trot. Negotiate each corner, go up the rail and transition to canter at B.

Go through the next corner, then turn down center line headed toward X (still in canter). BEFORE X, transition to walk (or trot if you are riding a young or less experienced horse). Take 3-5 walk strides, then transition back to canter, left lead. Do your best to stay straight through the canter transition and to the end of the ring!

Turn left at the rail, negotiate the corner in canter.

Trot at E.

This is the end of the pattern on this side.

Now you continue your trot around the rail until you go to B, at which point you canter, left lead. Everything will then flip around: you come off the rail at C, simple change through X, turn right at the rail and trot at E. I didn't draw out the flipped pattern to save space.

This is what I call a "running pattern." You can keep going several times through the pattern, and you will end up working on both reins (sides of the horse and rider). It's important to always mirror what you do on one side to the other side, so as to develop equal strength and suppleness on both sides.

VIII. LIGHTEN YOUR HORSE'S FOREHAND – FROM THE HIND END

Photo Credit: N. Banaszak

often watch riders pulling up on their reins to ask their horses to raise the head and neck. While we don't want the horse to trudge along with all their weight on their front legs, just pulling up on the rein is not the answer.

The horse might lift his neck in response to the discomfort in his mouth, but invariably, he drops it again within a few strides because a horse simply cannot lift the head and neck if the rest of the body is tending toward being on the forehand and strung out (not engaged in the hind end). He may try to please you by cranking his neck up, but that movement will only put more weight on the forelegs and tilt the horse's body more to the ground.

So how do you lighten the forehand, using the horse's "natural" biomechanics, especially in the late novice to beginning intermediate stages of training? Try this amazing transition exercise and see how your horse feels after several repetitions.

This exercise is a good one for several reasons:

First, it "tunes in" your horse to your aids, mainly because there are many things going on in succession. It also makes you stay active and balanced through the sequence of movements.

Second, it works on helping your horse bring his balance back to the hind end, while lightening the forehand.

Third, it requires more impulsion which in turn helps the horse round his back and strengthen over the topline.

Fourth, it adds "spice" to your flat work, which is nice for everyone!

Exercise
- Canter
- Trot
- Canter
- Walk

Start At Canter

Get to the canter, preferably from a walk. If a non-progressive transition is too advanced for you or your horse, do trot before the canter but make it as short as possible.

Canter several strides - let's say 20 strides. You can make it longer or shorter depending on your needs.

Transition to Trot

Once you have an active and rhythmical canter, do a downward transition to trot.

Do not stay in trot for long. Ideally, go back to the canter within three to five strides. If you can't make it that quickly, do as many strides as you need, but keep working toward three to five as a maximum.

Transition to Canter

Immediately ask for a new canter departure. If your horse slows down the canter tempo a little, accept it and slow your seat down too. You want to encourage any attempt your horse makes to "carry" rather than run. If his neck comes up, accept that too, because as he tucks his hind end under, his front end and neck will naturally elevate. Don't catch him in the mouth or pull on the reins or make him drop his head. Simply continue riding with the newly elevated forehand.

Transition to Walk

This one may be the most difficult, after all the energizing you just did. But it's well worth the effort.

Ideally, you would canter right to the walk, and then march out of the transition in a forward flowing, active walk. However, it might not happen that way for a while until your horse understands. He might trot before the walk, or fall heavily to the forehand as he lurches to a walk.

That is ok. Just keep trying, keep feeling for and adjusting your timing of the aids, and use half-halts in preparation for each downward transition.

Continue the sequence with a new transition to canter after 3-5 walk strides, and start it all over again.

Notes

It is easier for the horse to do this exercise on a large 20-meter (or bigger) circle to begin. As you get better at it, you can do the transitions on a straight line (more difficult). If you get really good, you can do it on a circle, then on a line, then change directions to a new circle - all the while, going through the transitions.

The key to this exercise is to minimize the trot and walk sections so that the horse's weight shifts back and frees up the front end. The canter encourages the hind end while the trot and walk help to prevent the horse from falling to the forehand.

You can change the sequence to keep things fresh:
- canter-walk-canter-walk,
- canter-walk-canter-trot,
- canter-trot-canter-trot.

It's really up to you, how your horse feels and what you want to get out of the exercise.

Keep in mind that this exercise is fairly taxing and requires a lot of muscular effort. If your horse isn't very fit, don't do too many in a row. Break it up with some walking or other low impact work before trying again, or do just a few each day for a while until your horse has a chance to build up stamina.

I like the canter-trot-canter-walk because of the walk at the end. It gives us a chance to gather ourselves up, take a breath and prepare again for the canter. I also think the walk-canter transition is very helpful in getting the horse to work from the hind end, which is always one of my major goals.

IX. SEVEN ESSENTIAL AIDS FOR AN EPIC CANTER TRANSITION

When you first learn to canter, it's about all you can do to get the horse to change his legs from a two-beat trot to a three-beat canter. You do pretty much anything you can to make the transition happen - lean forward, kick, kick harder, kick some more, let the reins go, use your voice....

You might feel like the canter is a huge speed-up from the trot, and when the horse finally does canter, the euphoric feeling of strength and power sends you into a rocking horse motion that just can't really be adequately described to the non-rider.

But then you get better at it.

You realize that the canter departure doesn't have to resemble a rocket launch. You develop your aids till both you and your horse look a lot more civilized - and a lot less frantic. At some point, you realize that you can trot, maintain the trot rhythm, and elegantly step into the canter. Your aids become invisible, prompting less educated onlookers to think that the horse is reading your mind.

So how exactly do you develop an epic canter transition? How do the aids become refined enough to create a smooth, balanced and active upward transition? In the following seven steps, I've tried to break down each component of the transition in order to explain the nuances that go into a split-second movement! Although it might seem a little complicated, I describe each moment that goes into a better developed canter departure.

Once you know each part that goes into the one movement, you might be able to problem-solve your departures with your horse and focus on one or two aspects as needed.

1. It All Starts With the Seat

Well, we already know this. But how does the seat exactly play into the transition? First off, your seat should be trotting when the horse is trotting. So if you are sitting the trot, your seat bones are actually moving in the rhythm of the trot. Be sure to promote a strong but not fast rhythm - one that your horse finds easy to move in while remaining supple.

If you are posting the trot, sit the last few strides before the canter. Use your seat to draw up the horse's hind legs, asking for more impulsion.

2. Use the Inside Leg/Outside Rein

The inside leg has a very important job in this moment. Apply the whole leg (from ankle up) at the girth to ask the horse for a mild bend to prepare for the inside lead. If your horse has a tendency to lean in just before the transition, your inside leg becomes even more critical in helping the horse maintain balance by not allowing him to drop his rib cage toward the middle of the ring.

The outside rein does little except to act as a "neck rein" - the one that sits onto the horse's neck and prevents him from drifting to the outside. It also can apply the half-halt aids before and after the departure.

3. Half-Halt Preparation

Do one or two or three half-halts *before* the transition.

We often tend to "throw everything away" (as in, lengthen the reins, take the legs off the horse, fall to the horse's front) as we head into the gait change. Fight that impulse and instead, keep the horse together. Keep your*self* together!

Falling to the forehand and trotting faster before the canter almost always ensures a low-quality canter gait. Although the horse might transition, he will likely be on the forehand, braced in his neck and jaw and hollow in his back. He will also likely trot sooner than later, no matter what you do to keep him going because he simply can't maintain his balance.

Instead, after you ask for impulsion, half-halt the horse to balance his weight to the hind end. Keep your legs on for impulsion after the half-halt.

4. Use the Outside Leg - Ask For the Lead

The outside leg initiates the lead. Some people call it a "windshield wiper" motion: swing your lower leg behind the girth to ask for the first stride. The horse's outside hind leg should strike off into the lead as your leg reaches back.

5. Canter with Your Seat

So far, your seat should have been trotting. Now, it needs to transition. So you go from two seat bones moving in tandem with the horse in the trot, to a canter motion with the inside seat bone leading (to allow for the horse to take the inside lead). Your seat now needs to promote the canter movement - swinging back and forth thanks to your supple lower back.

Keep your shoulders fairly still by moving *through* your back. The swinging movement allows for the *illusion* of your shoulders staying still while the horse is moving.

6. Use the Half-Halt Again

Just because the horse is now in canter doesn't mean that you should stop riding! Many of us tend to freeze in our aids, opting instead to just hang on to the increased movement of the canter. Well, as soon as you have enough balance and are able, ride actively again.

Half-halt - once, twice, three times maybe - in the rhythm of the canter. This helps the horse to stay "together" after the transition. The sudden surge of energy needs to be controlled so that it doesn't just fall on the horse's shoulders and forehand.

7. Canter on!

Now all you have to do is commit to the horse's movement. Your seat should allow the movement that your horse offers, and it's your job to not let your upper body fall forward or backward or sideways while your seat follows, follows and follows (unless you do another half-halt).

♦ ♦ ♦

When you first start paying attention to each of these aspects of the canter transition, you might need to actually think through every part, talking your body into the necessary activity while negotiating the canter movement. But rest assured - with practice and time, things become more and more automatic, and then you can focus more on your horse's specific needs.

Though we are talking about so many steps all subdivided here, in reality, it all comes together within a few seconds - from preparation, to the request, strike-off and follow-through. Eventually, it happens so seamlessly that the departure becomes just a quick thought - one that transpires between both you and your horse in an epic, seemingly mind-reading fashion!

X. HOW TO FINE-TUNE YOUR CANTER-TROT TRANSITIONS

The thing about riding in the canter is that at some point, you have to come out of it!

At first, the most basic way you can get a horse to transition down is by pulling on the reins. Most horses are kind enough to allow their legs to change gait at some point after they feel the pull on the reins.

The problem with just pulling on the reins to change gait is that you have to actually interfere with the movement of the horse. The horse reacts physically to the pull in several ways.

First off, he can't bring the inside hind leg underneath his body freely. Then he might have to lift his head to counterbalance the lack of stride length, which results in hollowing his back. The hollowness causes tension - which radiates through the back to the hips and to the neck.

The rider will likely feel the imbalance, possible coming into imbalance herself because she has already committed to the pulling action. She'll fall forward or backward depending on the force of the imbalance. The horse will obviously be stronger than the rider, thereby bracing more in the neck and jaw in order to continue forward into the trot.

Once the trot is achieved, both rider and horse will continue in that sort of tension.

But as with all things riding, it does get better than that. At some point, most of us find a better way - one that allows the horse his full freedom of movement while also getting the gait change and maintaining balance. We learn to fine tune our aids, enough so that it looks like (and sometimes feels like) we didn't do anything and the horse was a mind reader.

Here are the aids to help you fine tune your trot-canter transitions.

1. First, develop a strong canter before the transition.

Not a fast canter - amp up your horse's energy level just before you begin to apply your trot aids. This helps the horse reach further underneath his body with his inside hind leg (balance) so that he can support his weight from the hind end once his legs change.

2. Half-halt.

We've talked about how to half-halt before. In this case, the type of half-halt can vary depending on how strong you need to be. In my dreams, I always want to "whisper" my aids - and maybe use only the seat and minimal rein pressure. But in reality, I might need to be clearer than just a whisper. The idea is to use your aids as much as you need to, but as little as possible.

The advantage of using a half-halt as opposed to a rein pull is that there is regular release through the reins (even if it's not a let go of the reins). The horse won't feel a constant pull that he has to brace against. In fact, the inside rein might even "flutter" through the downward transition aids. Try it and see how your horse responds.

3. Trot.

At this point, your seat should be trotting. You can start posting as soon as your horse changes his legs (or sit into the trot motion).

4. Balance and go!

You'll need at least one, or maybe two or three half-halts right after the gait change. It depends on your horse's balance. If he maintains a level or uphill balance, then just one half-halt will help him stay that way. If he falls to the forehand, be there to support him until he can rebalance.

Make sure you don't fall forward. Make sure you don't get left behind! Stay strong in your core and move with the horse rather than against him.

The trot out of the canter can often be strong and powerful. In this case, don't stifle the horse's desire to move. Go with him and let him enjoy his balance and strength. This is often a great way to develop the horse's quality of trot and use of the hind end.

Some horses come to an almost stop. This would be the moment to urge your horse into a stronger trot. Don't chase him - just encourage and see what you get.

You can practice the "go!" after the downward transition several times until your horse feels freer and more willing/able to get into that powerful post-canter trot.

As with all skills in riding, you can try this sequence several times and work on developing your aids and your horse's responses. When you've done enough, leave it and come back to it another day.

XI. A STRETCH AND STRENGTHEN CANTER EXERCISE

N eed some "legging up" in canter?
Working in canter for an extended period of time (let's say, around 5 minutes) has many benefits. The exercise below is an awesome way to develop (you and) your horse's conditioning, work on suppling the horse over the back in canter, play around with balance and hind end engagement, and just work toward something as simple as maintaining a steady tempo.

This exercise is also good if you find that your horse often drops his back (and "giraffe necks") when you transition to canter, or during the canter. We want to teach the horse to loosen through the back and allow it to move while in canter.

Use the whole arena for this, with circles at A and C. Try to do this in an easy pace - not too fast, not too slow.

You can always build up the horse's impulsion as he settles and begins to use himself better, without adding speed to it.

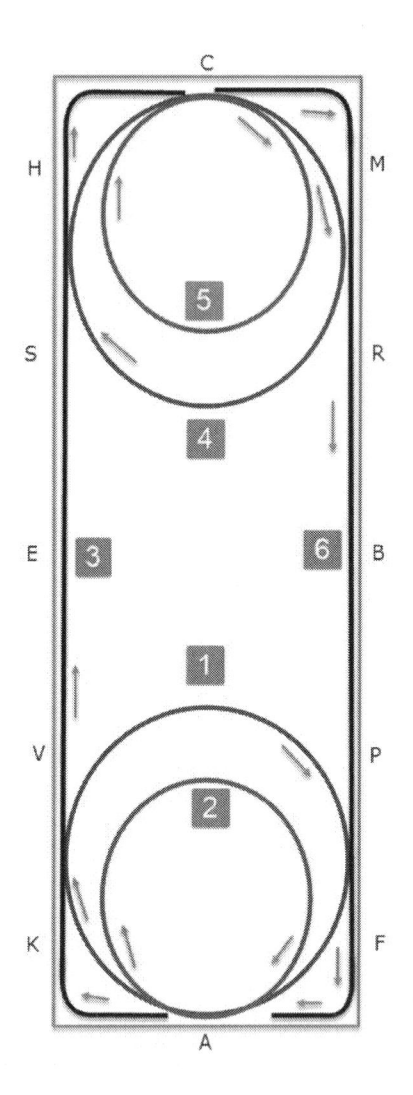

The pattern sounds like it isn't much work, but there's quite a lot going on when you go around a few times and let it work you and your horse.

Start at A. Canter on the right rein.

1. 20-m circle

Start with an easy, softly stretching 20-m circle. Think of it as a half-stretch, so not really stretching down as you would for say, a 2nd level dressage test. But do make it a stretch, so that your horse can carry his head a little lower than usual, and stretch through the back a little more than usual.

Ride in half-seat yourself, and take most of your weight off the horse's back.

Keep a mild 20-m bend, keeping your horse on a large circle but watching the outside shoulder. Keep the shoulder straight and allow the bend to happen through the body, not just through the neck.

2. 10-m circle

When you get back to A, do another circle, this time much smaller. Make it a 10-m circle, with more bend, and sit into the saddle and bring the horse up into a nice uphill outline. This circle requires more collection, so keep the canter active and strong but add in the deeper 10-m bend.

3. Canter on up the long side of the rail

After the 10-m circle, head into the corner and then go straight up along the rail. Go back to the half-seat, and ask your horse for the small stretch again, this time on the straight rail. The long side of the ring should allow you plenty of time to strengthen the canter (not speed up, though) and develop a nice, even tempo and stride length.

Strengthen: If your horse feels good, isn't pulling down on the reins, and feels like he has good balance, ask for a little longer stride and a little more impulsion. Don't let the reins go longer and make sure you ease the horse into the bigger movement. (If your horse does pull down on the reins, just sit up a little and ease up on the canter, or even do a down transition to trot, and then canter on again. We want the horse to strengthen the canter, but not to end up on the forehand. So use trot transitions to bring the horse into balance again, as needed.)

You're feeling for a bouncier, more trampoline-y canter. You should also feel like you spend more time in the air than on the ground.

4. 20-m circle

Go through the next corner and back to a 20-m circle at C. Stay in the half-seat for the 20-m circle, and keep the horse in the mild stretch. The difference between the stretch here and on the rail is that you have to re-establish a bend (even though it's just a mild bend) so you're also working on the lateral suppleness on this circle.

5. 10-m circle

Now do a 10-m circle at C. Sit, prepare for the bend as you come back to C, and then bring the horse uphill again in his outline. Use this circle to let your horse do a little "carrying", have a higher and shorter outline, and use his now more active hind end to take some weight off the forehand.

6. Canter down the long side of the rail

Then ease out of the 10-m circle through the corner and down the next rail in the half-stretch (for him) and half-seat (for you) position again.

And repeat! If you want, you can do this pattern several times in a row one way, and then take a walk break, and do it several times the other way.

You can also do the whole thing in walk and trot, either as a warm-up or as a cool-down. The concept of stretching and then shortening the back is a great way to supple and strengthen the horse's back and hind end in all gaits.

XII. BOLD TRANSITIONS THAT LOOK EFFORTLESS AND FEEL GREAT

This one is good for the horses that tend to "suck back" before transitions and/or "run out" after the transitions.

There are transitions and then there are Transitions. The good ones are precise, strong and balanced. They are so clear and easily done that it looks like the rider didn't do anything. The horse stays round, energetic and bold. The gait change is matter-of-fact, *easy*. In fact, good transitions are critical for a seamless, harmonized ride.

The opposite is easily obvious to the onlooker. Poorly executed transitions are sluggish and slow to develop. The horse seems to labor through the transition, the rider has to use obvious aids and still it takes time to get the gait change. The horse hollows his back, falls further to the forehand and maybe stumbles or runs through the rider's aids. The rider might struggle to keep balance through the lurches until the gait change finally happens.

For the purposes of this exercise, the word "transition" can mean several changes:
- upward or downward progressive transitions (walk to trot, canter to trot).
- upward or downward non-progressive transitions (walk to canter, trot to halt).
- change of direction (trot from the left to the right).
- straight line to turn (change of direction across the diagonal to a left turn into the corner).

Exercise

We often talk about it but we often forget to actually do it. *Every* transition can benefit from it. There is nothing more important for it.

What is it?

Energy. Impulsion. *Oomph*.

It actually sounds simple. All you need to do is ask for a little more energy before and after the transition. Let's try it with a progressive, upward transition.

Let's say you are trotting to the left and want to pick up a canter after the next corner. This is a good way to encourage a young horse to canter as the helps to balance, and the horse sees all the space ahead of him as he comes out of the corner.

As you approach the corner, you feel your horse slow down momentarily. This is quite normal, especially if you are riding in an indoor arena - the horse backs off a bit when he's faced with the walls that appear to come at him. A more trained horse understands that he is going to turn through the corner and have the long side ahead.

1. Your "oomph" moment occurs a few strides before the transition. Use both your legs for energy and lighten your seat to allow the energy over the back.
2. Then do a small half-halt before asking for the gait change.
3. Ask for the canter.

4. Once the horse is cantering, ask for another energy surge.
5. Use another half-halt afterward to not allow the horse to just run out from under you.

You see what I mean. It's basically like you are strengthening both your body (in terms of tone and energy) and your horse's movement as you go into and out of the transition.

Done well, there will be no obvious lurch or energy surge. In fact, the remarkable result will be that it looks like nothing happened at all, except a fluidity of movement, a calm, relaxed tempo, lack of conflict and confident, bold movement. Think connection, steady, consistency.

The reason this happens is that the horse *won't* slow every few strides, won't break stride and have to change gait again and won't have to go through the resultant imbalances. The rider won't kick the horse every few strides, won't wait for the gait change and then have to recover and won't be lurched in the saddle again and again.

At first, it might seem like you're asking for energy many times before and after the transition. You're right - you probably are! It will take time for you and your horse to become accustomed to the amount of energy it takes to move freely through the many changes we require over the course of a ride. After a while, it simply becomes second nature to prepare and complete all changes this way. Once you get used to doing it yourself, your horse will likely be right there with you with no hint of suck back or run out. Because as you know, all riding problems start and end with the rider!

Next time you ride, give this a try. Those five steps above happen very quickly in rapid succession, so prepare ahead of time and know what you're going to do before you go through with it. Maybe have someone on the ground to help be your eyes and tell you how the horse looks to, through and after the transition.

SECTION 4: SUPPLENESS

19. LEG YIELD/ SHOULDER-FORE – A GREAT WAY TO YOUR HORSE'S BACK

We know why we want a supple back.
Think of the back as the gateway to all things good in horse riding. A supple back allows energy through the horse's top line. It releases tension, loosens muscles - allows instead of blocks. The up-and-down action of the back creates space for the hind legs to reach underneath the body, which will in turn promote better balance - whether on a turn or straight line.

But most importantly, the supple back allows the horse to carry you, the rider, in a more healthy fashion. Which is something we should all be interested in.

Consider the opposite: the clenched, unmoving back. Tightness. Rigidity. Blockage. Hind legs out behind the horse's center of gravity. Lack of balance. Bracing neck and on the forehand.

That image should be motivation enough to make you want to put in the effort it might take to learn how to get the horse to "work through the back."

While there is definitely much more to the supple back, the exercise below can help you get started at a basic level. These two movements combine to give you a sort of road map, if you will, to begin to find your horse's back.

1. Start with the leg yield.

Do it on a circle, in trot.

Use your inside leg at the girth, and stay evenly balanced in the saddle. Leg yield outward so that the circle becomes a little bit larger, bit by bit. The idea is to get the horse to lift through the rib cage (in response to your leg), lift the inside shoulder and shift weight to the outside. The horse's legs may or may not cross over each other - in this exercise, the cross-over is not required. Just a shift to the outside is fine, especially at the beginning.

You might notice that it is somewhat easier to get a bend to the inside if you can get the leg yield going well. The horse will already be reaching underneath the body deeper with the inside hind leg, and will be able to maintain better balance into the bend. Without too much fuss happening from your hands, you should feel the bend, mostly thanks to your leg aid.

So now, your horse is stepping outward and the inside bend is developing.

Enjoy this for a few strides. Lighten your contact at this point, lighten your seat, and allow more energy through the horse's body while still stepping out and bending.

You're looking for a bouncier feeling, a swingier back... basically, more freedom of movement and energy.

Once you feel you have a nice bend and some easy steps outward, you might find that your outside rein "fills up" on its own, and suddenly, you have this wonderful neck rein on the outside rein, which will naturally lead you right into #2.

2. Shoulder-Fore

Now that you've activated the hind end, you can see if the front end can become lighter and straighter.

The shoulder-fore is a basic but excellent way to line up the horse's front end so that it leads slightly to the inside (and works on the bend again).

Using your outside neck rein, bring your horse's shoulders just a little ahead of the hind leg tracks. In other words, the horse's front leg tracks should fall slightly to the inside of the hind leg tracks.

> *How to shoulder-fore:*
> *1. Position your body on the bend to the inside, with your seat weighted slightly to the inside, inside leg at the girth, outside leg behind the girth and rein aids following your shoulders toward the circle.*
> *2. Feel for the horse's shoulders. They should feel slightly off-set to the inside.*

At this point, the novice horse tends to want to fall into the middle of the circle. It is the job of your inside leg, seat bone and rein to keep the horse on the curve. Your outside rein can also help to keep the straightness by half-halting to counter the horse's momentum toward the inside. It can also keep the neck fairly straight, even while bending.

Get a friend to monitor your horse's foot falls and let you know about the angle of the horse's body. She should tell you when you have it right so that you can memorize what it feels like to have straightness in your horse's movements.

You're still on the circle, you just did the leg yield out, developed a bit of a bend, and now, using the outside neck rein and outside leg behind the girth, you bring the shoulders back in towards the middle of the circle - just a little.

If the leg yield was going to create a bulging outside shoulder, this shoulder-fore will quickly avoid the problem altogether. You'll notice that the outside shoulder straightens up a little and the front end lightens a little.

The straightening action will align the horse's spine and once again, you'll feel the trampoline-y feeling of the back that is active, round and engaged.

When You Get Good

Try it on one side first, then the other.

Then, switch sides - go right, then left, then right. Go off the circle and make it fun by finding new turns and circles in different places in the arena. Use serpentines, tear drops, S-changes... get creative!

Common Problems

When you first start with the leg yield, many horses will misunderstand the leg aid to mean speed up. If your horse quickens the legs instead of steps out, half-halt the speed, and regain your initial tempo. Then try again. It may take many repetitions for a horse to learn to step sideways away from a leg aid. Be patient, clear and reward often.

Another common problem is that the horse will continue to lean into your leg as you apply the leg aid. Many horses naturally lean into pressure. If your horse leans into your leg, come to a walk. Apply your leg aid again, and get the horse to leg yield at the walk. When the horse is responding, go back to trot.

While finding your horse's swinging back might be a difficult challenge, the feeling of floating energy that comes with suppleness is something you'll never want to go without ever again after you've found it for the first time. The bonus is that if you can listen carefully enough, you will realize that your horse appreciates it too!

20. GO WITH THE HORSE

It sounds simple, doesn't it?

Just go with the horse.

Isn't that what you're supposed to do? I mean, if you're on the horse's back, and the horse is moving, you're undoubtedly going along with him (unless you're off his back and on the ground - fairly undesired).

So what's the fuss about "go"ing with the horse?

The novice rider, of course, can attest to how difficult it can be to learn to move with the horse. The rider's entire body has to learn the up-and-down and forward-back sways to the various gaits. It's not like picking up a tennis racket and learning to hit a ball (as hard as that may be initially); it's your *whole body*.

After a while, though, it gets easier and you learn to "stick" in the saddle better and you sway merrily along in tandem with your horse. But still, there's more to the going than just that.

The fact is, we will hone our "go with the horse" skills for years and years to come.

When Should You Go With The Horse?

While we often speak of half-halts and transitions to maintain balance and prevent the horse from running heavily to the forehand, there are many moments during a ride when we should make significant attempts to get out of the horse's way, so to speak, and let him do his thing while we do our best to avoid interfering and being a hindrance.

These are the moments when we just flow along in the horse's movement. We neither augment the movement nor stifle it.

Harmonize

Think of two dance partners as they step and twirl across the dance floor. They both move as one, and this is what we must do in many riding instances.

Impulsion

Pushing power - that's when you've asked the horse to move along in response to your leg and/or seat aids. You've asked for increased energy, and the horse obliged by bounding ahead in the movement. In these cases, you just ride that wave of energy and let the horse know that you can be a partner in his larger movement. You can always go to the half-halt a few strides later - but after the initial ask, you should "just go."

Encourage the horse

This can be done when the horse takes initiative to offer something you weren't expecting.

Reinforce the right answer.
After he makes an attempt at what you've asked, then surely, you can just ride along for a few strides to let him know he's on the right track.

Develop confidence.
"Just go" after the horse has overcome a mentally or physically demanding task (such as ride past a spooky corner) - get out of the horse's way and let him do his thing.

Here's How
It's a simple concept: allow your body to move with the horse. But let's break it down a bit for the sake of clarity.

1. Loosen through the lower back
Many of us need to teach our lower backs to move with the horse, especially if we start riding in our adult years. Tight ligaments and tendons contribute to the body simply not being able to move enough with the horse, so one of our initial goals must be to be able to move through the lower back and seat.

2. Soften the elbows
Sometimes, it's useful to just loosen through the elbows. We often maintain tight elbows (and shoulders) in attempt to maintain adequate balance and connection. If you find yourself being a little too clutch-y, focus on loosening through the elbows. Avoid letting the reins get longer, and avoid the opposite - pulling backward on the reins. Instead, find the feeling of just loosening within a consistent rein length so that the horse can find a release but doesn't become suddenly unbalanced either way.

3. "Swing" through your body

Think of this as letting your horse move your body. You kind of trampoline along with him - with adequate tone - so that you become light and buoyant within his movement. Just remember that it's not like becoming complete jelly. Too much flop becomes a hindrance for the horse as well as allows you to lose balance.

4. Travel further

If you're on the right track and your horse actually reaches further and strides out (rather than just speeds up his legs), you might find that you're being left behind. Your horse will feel you and stop his movement. Prepare for the energy surge. Make sure your shoulders stay above your hips (might require a very small lean back in preparation) and get ready to travel further with each stride.

While it may take many repetitions of just going every time you learn a new movement, it surely is worth the time spent. OK! Get out there and just go!

21. THREE STEPS TO A QUIETER LEG POSITION

Do any of these things happen to you?
You lose your stirrups during a transition.
You feel your feet bouncing in the stirrups, especially during sitting trot.
Your lower legs sway in canter.
You can't feel your feet in the stirrups.
You have trouble placing your legs on your horse's sides.
You can have nice long legs riding without stirrups, but still lose the stirrups as soon as you start using them again.

These things happen to most riders at some point, particularly during the first few years of riding. Sometimes, you develop a habit that lasts even longer, mostly because your body blueprinted itself long ago and now it's even more difficult to break that habit.

But it can be done.

We are always striving to maintain quieter legs, a more secure seat, and stable feet (preferably with the heels lower than the toes). The thing is, the harder we try to keep the legs from moving, the more they swing, tighten, and finally slide out of the stirrups!

What to do?

Here are three steps (pun intended!) to a quieter leg position.

1. Soften through the seat.

Whenever you find tension in the lower legs or feet, you can direct your attention higher up. In this case, consider your seat. Are you tight through the lower back? Are you gripping with the gluteal muscles? Maybe your hip angle is closed or you're leaning forward in the upper body.

In all these cases, start with softening through your seat. Don't become a blob of jelly – just feel for tension or gripping, and release that as much as you can. Allow the hip angle to open. Allow your upper thighs to really sit into the saddle.

Try to be quiet in your seat aids. If you feel you are moving bigger than your horse, or if you are pumping through your seat and body to get him moving, work toward whispering your aids, reducing body movement, and becoming lighter over the horse's back. We often get "too loud" in attempt to be clear. The quieter you can be in your body, the more opportunity you can have to feel your legs and the horse's sides.

So start with a softer seat that allows a more open hip angle and a straighter leg from the highest point of the thighs.

2. Straighten the leg from the hip through the knee down to the ankle.

Do two things with your leg.

First, rotate your leg inward toward the saddle, so your knee is facing straight ahead. You might need to grab the back of your riding breech and actually pull your leg slightly backward from the hip, placing the thigh flat on the saddle.

Second, straighten your knee slightly. Don't push it down too straight, but see how much you can open the knee angle as you lengthen your leg downward.

It's like a stretch of the leg, constrained within the length of your stirrup leathers. You might discover that your leg will naturally feel longer.

3. Push into the stirrup with your foot, allowing the heel to go down *if it can*.

Now let's focus on the foot itself.

The ball of your foot should be flat on the widest part of the stirrup. If placed correctly, you will feel like the stirrup is as solid as the ground. We call this "grounding" your feet in the stirrup.

After you have lengthened your leg in step 2, you might feel that your heel just wants to go down on its own. This is a great sign that you are on the right track. However, don't force your heels down - that would cause more tension in your leg and be counterproductive. Let the heel hang if it will.

Start at the halt.

Take time and soften through the seat and hip, position the leg and then ground the foot on each side. Do all of this at the halt first, so you can feel the effects on your seat and leg before you add movement.

Then try to maintain the leg position through each gait. Walk is easiest. It might take some effort at first but will feel more natural over time, until you aren't even aware that you are doing it.

The longer leg and softer muscles will also allow your seat to position deeper into the saddle.

One last thought. You might not be able to do all three steps right away. In fact, you might be able to do one, then another, then maybe two at a time... you know what I mean. Add transitions, the sitting trot or canter to the mix, and you might have to be even more patient.

So be aware of what your seat and legs feel like, work on loosening the seat and lengthening the leg, and one day, you might be surprised that somehow, without forcing anything, your legs stopped swaying, your stirrups stayed on your feet, and you can actually feel the stability of the stirrups even as you canter merrily along!

22. SUPPLING FUN! AN EXERCISE

Suppleness is one of those more difficult concepts to explain. Because it relates to "feel", it's one of those things in horse riding that takes a long time to learn to identify and then produce regularly.

To recap, suppleness happens in two ways in the horse's body - longitudinally and laterally.

Longitudinal suppleness refers to how loose and round the horse is over his back. It also relates to how "through" his energy is. If he holds his muscles in tight tension, or he blocks forward energy as you ask for more from your legs, he is likely not "through" and soft over the back.

Lateral suppleness refers to the side-to-side dexterity of the horse. It is involved in achieving good balance around turns, and in the horse's ability to bend. Both types of suppleness are also involved in the establishment of "connection": that ever elusive goal of becoming "one", or riding in harmony, with the horse. No matter what discipline you ride, softness over the back and left and right are basic, fundamental qualities of good (and healthy) movement.

It All Comes Down To You

Here's the thing. Even when I'm explaining what the horse is (or isn't) doing, it's not really about the horse. It's really all about you. The rider has to learn *how* to achieve the suppleness that is required and desired. Developing suppleness comes from the seat, the legs, the hands, the torso (= core strength) and quick coordination of all those aids. In fact, one could say that the rider needs to be supple enough to develop the horse's suppleness!

Exercise

Here is today's exercise. I like this one because it can help set you up to "find" suppleness just by virtue of riding through the pattern. You have to be sharp on this one - change your aids quickly to help the horse change the bend, go forward to an upward transition and then to a downward transition.

Do this exercise after you and your horse have had a good chance to warm up. This can be the "lesson" part of your ride, and be sure to listen carefully to your horse in order to not overwork him too long.

It's a fun exercise because it keeps you hopping, and it really feels nice and flowing once you get a hang of it. The energy is forward but you can't let it go all out "the front end" because then you won't be able to navigate the lateral suppleness that is required to complete the pattern. There are several changes of direction and transitions involved. I've divided the pattern into three parts just for ease of explanation. They all run concurrently.

Horse Listening

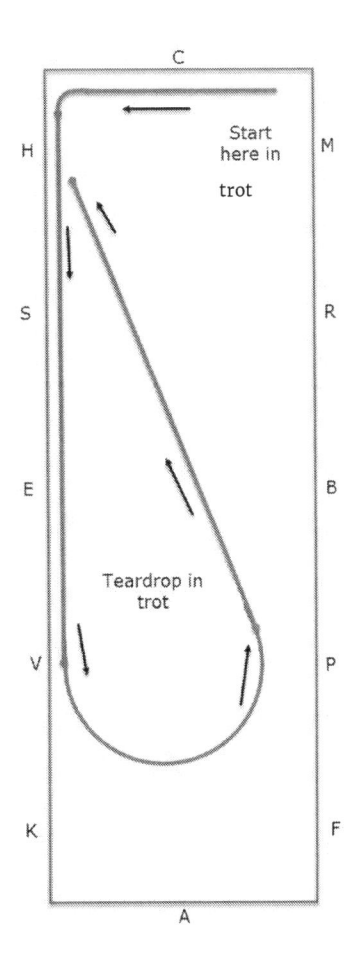

Part 1

1. Start on the rail to the left at trot.

2. Come off the rail before the end of the next corner and proceed to do a teardrop to the left. Make the turn fairly large (approx. 15 meters) so your horse has plenty of energy coming out of the turn and into the straight diagonal line. Prepare for change of bend for the corner that is coming up.

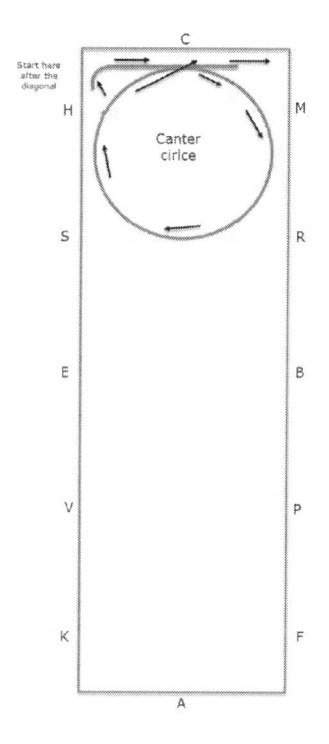

Part 2

3. Bend right, turn right through the corner. You can slightly shorten your horse's strides just before the bend to help him control the forward energy coming off the diagonal line.

4. At C: transition to a canter circle, right lead. Make this a smaller circle if your horse is more advanced, otherwise keep it larger and work on maintaining good energy through the whole circle. Transition back to trot before reaching C again.

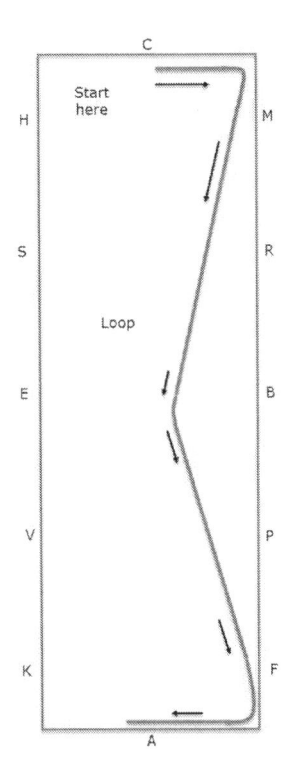

Part 3

5. Navigate the next corner, preparing for the upcoming loop.

6. Do a loop coming out of the corner. Notice the diagram shows a fairly narrow loop, meaning that you don't have to go all the way to X at the middle. Gauge the depth of the loop based on your horse's riding level. A straight loop is generally easier.

Start with a right bend, straighten for 2-3 strides over the middle of the loop, bend left to go back to the rail, and bend right again just before heading into the next corner. The loop can be tricky because it requires a bend to a bend to a bend!

This is the end of the pattern because now you will be on the right rein, heading into the next corner.

Keep Going!

Now you can start all over in the new direction. Your canter circle will be on A this time. The teardrop and the loop will end up being on the same side of the ring, regardless of the direction you're going in.

This exercise is designed to give you opportunity to focus on your aids - over and over again! As you get better at the pattern, see if you can sort of "dance" through the direction and gait changes. The idea is to subtly navigate the direction and gait changes while staying on the pattern. Keep up your horse's energy level but don't let him go too fast.

You're looking for keeping good balance as you negotiate each part of the pattern. You may find your horse softening over the back, left to right, and becoming bouncier. If he offers to slow his legs slightly but stay strong and forward in his gait, you know you're definitely on the right track! Make sure you do the same.

23. THIRY-EIGHT MOMENTS TO HALF-HALT

What does it feel like to get on your young horse's back for the first time?
Excitement.
Anticipation.
Nervousness!
If you've owned him since he was a foal, you might have waited two, three or four years before the breathtaking moment!
From that very first ride, to the subsequent weeks of awkward walk, to trot and finally canter - and then for the rest of the horse's *life* - there is really one thing that needs to be managed at all times while under saddle.
You guessed it: the horse's balance.
Which of course also includes your balance. In fact, everything we do on top of that horse will affect his balance, so we have to be equally obsessed with our own balance even while we help him maintain his.

Balance is a major issue for many reasons:

Physical: Lack of balance can cause all sorts of harm to the horse in the long term. Think of leg and tendon injuries, stumbling, back pain and so much more.

Mental: Sensitive horses especially react to lack of balance. Note the horse's expression when he is on the forehand or tight and tense through the back. Of course, there are more subtle signs like teeth grinding or pinned ears.

Rider Discomfort: Finally, the rider should be able to actually feel the imbalance, whether through uncomfortable movement, jarring through the gaits or general all-over body tension which creates the "cardboard back" that is difficult to sit to.

So how can you maintain balance, you ask?

The half-halt.

When do we need to apply the half-halt? If we are interested in preserving balance while we ride the horse, it all comes down to the timing.

Time the half-halt correctly *during* the horse's movement. In general, you want to time your aids while the inside hind leg is up off the ground (so the leg is free to move).

Also, time the half-halt so it occurs *between* the various movements. Many people say you should ride "half-halt to half-halt" - as in, the half-halts begin and end each and every movement (= changes of balance). If you think this must mean that you are constantly using half-halts, you're right!

When exactly should you balance (rebalance/catch the energy/give a "heads up")?

Here are 38 moments in a ride that you could use the half-halt.
1. Before the walk to halt
2. After the halt to walk
3. Before/after the trot to walk
4. Before/after the canter to trot
5. Before/after the trot to canter
6. Before/after the walk to trot
7. Before a corner in the ring
8. After a corner in the ring
9. Before a turn
10. After a turn
11. Before a circle begins
12. Halfway through the circle
13. Before the circle ends
14. A few strides after the circle
15. Before the "sit down" in trot/canter
16. After the "sit down" in trot/canter
17. Before a change of direction
18. After a change of direction
19. Before going into a straight line
20. Halfway through the straight line
21. After the straight line, in preparation for the next movement
22. Before going downhill
23. While going downhill
24. Before positioning into the shoulder-in/ haunches in
25. During the shoulder-in/haunches-in
26. After the shoulder-in/haunches-in

27. Before the leg yield/half-pass
28. During the leg yield/half-pass (especially to help the hind end catch up with the front end)
29. After the leg yield/half-pass
30. Before a spook
31. During a spook
32. Any time to refocus attention
33. Before an increase in engagement
34. After an increase in engagement
35. Any time to regain balance
36. Before any new movement
37. Before slowing down the tempo (regardless of gait)
38. Before speeding up the tempo (regardless of gait)

♦ ♦ ♦

I considered leaving out the "before" and "after" qualifiers but then I decided I wanted to make it very specific. We tend take the half-halt for granted and use it sometimes while forget about it at other times. In this case, I wanted to highlight the frequency that it needs to be used - basically, before and after *everything*!

Which brings us back to the first ride on the young horse. Even while he is finding his feet and learning about gaits, gait changes and what our aids mean, it is our responsibility to help him maintain the best balance possible during each phase of his education. Introduce the half-halt fairly early in his riding career and keep using it through all of his riding life!

24. GET RID OF THAT TENSION: FOUR STEPS TO IMPROVED SUPPLENESS

Suppleness can be an elusive concept for many people as well as horses. On the one hand, "finding" suppleness can be a rather long term and difficult undertaking, especially for novice horses or riders. On the other, suppleness is the key to all good movement. Without suppleness, you and your horse are left to always ride in tension and with a counterproductive posture.

Each component listed below takes time to learn and develop. In fact, you will likely need to go through these steps every time you learn something new with your horse. Every new skill will cause a certain amount of tension until both you and your horse figure out how to do the movement with better balance and impulsion.

I use these steps to help me stay focused on what needs to be done when. In other words, you can't go to increase the energy if you haven't found a clear rhythm yet. Do this for every single movement - a simple trot circle, or a walk pirouette, a lengthen or a half pass. It doesn't really matter what you're doing. Just work on each component of the movement in this order, and work towards reducing tension and improving suppleness.

1. Rhythm

First off, find rhythm. Pay attention to your horse's footfalls. Is he doing a clear 2-beat in the trot? Can you hear an even 1,2,3 - suspension in the canter? Listen closely, feel for the footfalls, and make sure the rhythm is crystal clear.

If you hear muddled footsteps, take note of your aids. Maybe you need to strengthen or lighten your seat aids, or use more leg for better impulsion. Maybe you need to slow down a bit to allow your horse enough time for each footfall.

In each case, focus on finding a good rhythm for your horse. He should be able to maintain it, regularly, for several strides. Don't go on to Step 2 until you have a clear, strong rhythm.

2. Energy

Next, work on energy level. There are times when almost all horses need to increase energy. It might happen as you come into a corner, or when you are turning on a small circle. Your horse might "suck back" in a lateral movement like a shoulder-in or leg yield. The idea is to get the rhythm first, then recognize when your horse is letting the energy "out the back end."

Use your legs and follow with your seat. Ask your horse for more energy, which should translate into bigger strides and a rounder back. If your horse flattens and just rushes along, use half-halts to rebalance. Make sure you have rhythm, then ask for energy all over again.

3. Longitudinal Flexion

Once you have rhythm and energy, you can focus on getting your horse to move "over the back." The energy you now have can be transferred over the back to allow your horse to round better. Half-halts help a lot, but equally important is your seat and upper body balance. Try to stay with the horse's movement (don't get left behind) and then lighten your seat (tighten your buttocks) so that you don't inadvertently stop the energy in the saddle area.

Ride the energy, go with the forward motion, and then use your half-halts to keep your horse's balance from falling to the forehand.

4. Lateral Flexion

After you have the horse moving over the back, you can focus on side-to-side flexion and bend. I find that once the horse finds longitudinal flexion, he'll flex laterally much more easily than if he was tight over the back. So first, you must have rhythm, energy and roundness.

Then work on the sides. You can ask for a mild flex to the inside (or outside too) using just your upper body position and light contact. Or you can work on a true bend using your seat, leg aids and upper body and hands.

When bending, make sure you don't overbend - a 20-meter circle or turn has only a mild bend. Increase the amount of bend as your circle gets smaller. But make sure you bend through the body, not just the neck. Your leg, seat, upper body and hands should be also bent according to your circle.

Use the outside rein to prevent an overbend but use your inside leg and seat to create the bend in the first place. Be sure to have mini-releases on your inside rein (make the rein "flutter") so you don't take steady pressure and prevent the inside hind leg from coming under the body.

There are surely many other ways to improve your horse's suppleness but I find this method works well, especially if you are riding without an instructor. You can just go through each part in your mind.

As you get better at it, you'll go through each step fairly quickly. In fact, you might get through all four steps within 2-3 strides of your horse. Do you have rhythm? Great, then get some energy. Enough energy? Then let the energy come over the back. Enough roundness? Then let's work on bend.

Final note: I find that as you go through these steps with your horse, your *own* tension starts to dissipate as well. For some people, breaking down the steps helps a lot to focus their intention. Other people might want to keep things more cohesive, and try to get it all together at the same time.

In all cases, listen to your horse. Look for a rounder, swingier movement. Listen for snorts and deep breaths. Feel for lightness, better balance and maybe even floppy ears!

SECTION 5: COLLECTION

25. THE MANY USES OF THE OVAL

Ride the circle but don't diss the oval!
The oval is rarely talked about in dressage circles (see the pun?) but it can be used quite successfully for many purposes. While a circle is helpful in establishing a bend and encouraging better use of the horse's hind end, the oval offers something that the circle does not: the straight line that occurs in between two turns.

If you want to throw a little line into your circles, the oval is a great option. The horse has to learn to not only bend and adjust the hind end activity for the circle, but then he can use that increased activity to take into a line. The line allows the horse the opportunity to move more forward, increase the stride length and reach ahead. Think expansion after compaction.

Then comes the next turn. Back to engagement of the hind end, bending, and using the inside hind leg deeper under the body.

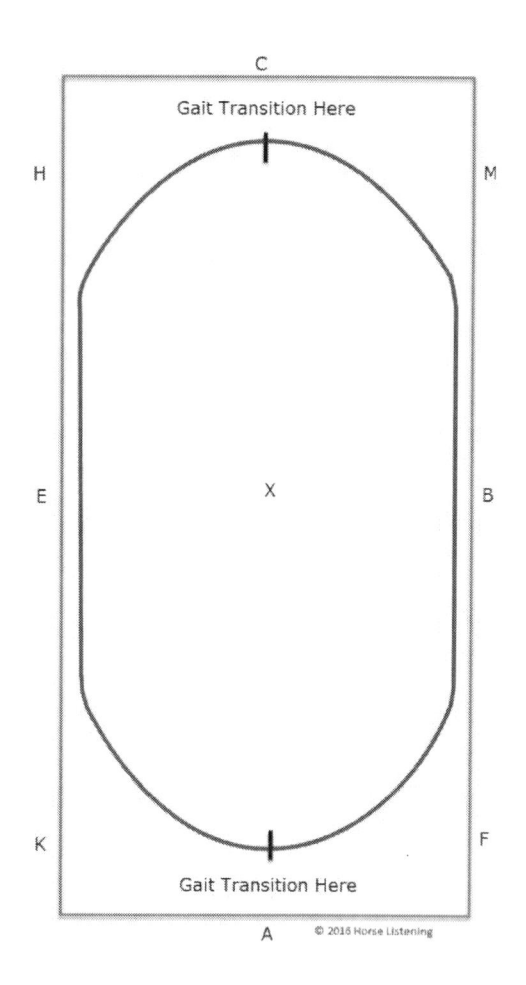

Exercise

Try this exercise for some challenging balance and transition development.

Transition points are in the middle of each turn section.

Start with a trot as you come out of the turn into the straight line. Go up the line at trot (probably should use a shoulder-fore to ensure straightness).

Begin the next turn in trot. Transition to canter in the middle of the turn.

Finish the next turn and head into the straight line in canter. Transition back to trot in the middle of the new turn.

Keep going! Do it a few times, then you can take a walk break and change directions.

If you want to increase difficulty, do walk-canter transitions.

If you think you're ready for it, try canter-counter-canter transitions through walk (as in, canter in the true lead for half the oval, and counter canter in the other half).

Possible Problems and Corrections

Correct ovals can be difficult to master, considering the various balance shifts and bend changes. If you can be aware of potential problems, you can help support your horse through the oval to help him (and you!) maintain the best balance he can as he goes through the exercises.

Crookedness

The oval is a great tool to show you just how straight you and your horse really are. Any drifting, falling in, or shoulder-bulging will become very evident as you negotiate the end of a turn and head into the straight line.

Horse drifts out: Use a strong enough (as much as needed, as little as possible) neck rein to keep your horse's shoulders moving on the turn and not drifting out. You can add outside leg to help keep the hips on the line and a mild open rein on the inside rein to invite the shoulders a bit to the inside (shoulder-fore) if needed.

Horse falls in: Use an open inside rein combined with your inside leg and seat bone to push the horse outward.

Shoulder-Bulging: By this, I mean that the horse leans (or "falls") on one shoulder or the other. It can happen on the inside shoulder or the outside, depending on the crookedness of the horse, even if the horse still moves in a straight line. In either case, ride with two direct reins (with contact but *not pulling*), hands in front of the saddle by the withers, and don't let the horse take the reins away from you. Stabilize yourself through strong elbows on your body and tight core, and you can stabilize the horse too.

Add some leg for impulsion and get the horse to straighten thanks to the forward energy.

Speeding Up On the Line

Many horses will have a tendency to go faster after they round the final part of the turn. The extra energy and strength achieved by the turn will prompt them to speed up their legs and head off into the sunset! Beware of that extra tempo, because extra speed invariably means falling to the forehand.

You can't let all the energy just fly out the "front door", so to speak. This is where half-halts are essential in helping to keep the horse balanced and moving uphill as much as possible. Maintain the leg speed by half-halting even as you turn the last corner before the straight line. Then half-halt as needed as you straighten.

Your horse will begin to predict the balance control after you do this a few times. Always remember - you don't want the leg speed to increase. If anything, you want the stride length to increase. Not the speed!

"Sucking Back" on the Turn

The opposite can happen as you come into a turn. Your horse might actually disengage in the hind end - shorten his stride, hollow his back a bit, slow down... he might leave his hind end out behind him. You might actually feel like he becomes more comfortable as he moves *less* and stops swinging through the back.

It's perfectly reasonable for a horse to do this as he enters a turn, because negotiating a turn off a straight line takes work and strength. In this case, you will need to be aware and feel it coming on. Use both legs to encourage your horse forward, and use your reins to prepare for the bend and turn aids.

Again, you're not trying to get your horse to launch off to oblivion, but you are working on maintaining the energy you acquired on the straight line.

Using the Rail for the Turn

This is generally a rider problem. Sure, the horse might want to drift to the rail, but the track the horse takes is always determined by the rider.

Because it's a rider problem, it can be easily fixed! Make sure that you turn off the rail early, not at the end of your ring. Teach your horse that he can come off the rail at any point on the line. Then head to the opposite rail.

You can also work on staying a few feet off the rail itself when you're on the straight line. Practice teaching the horse to move straight on his own, not using the rail for direction. If you have a large ring, this can be easily done. It's harder to do in a small ring, but you can make a point of staying off the rail even a little in that case.

26. CRYSTAL CLEAR ABOUT CANTER LEADS & A QUICK FIX

Are you crystal clear on your canter leads? Do you know which one is which and when you need to change leads?

It happens to everyone at some point in their riding journey, horse and human alike.

The whole idea of staying on the "correct" lead is important in riding development. The main reason we worry about leads is to maintain balance, especially on turns and circles. If the horse is on the "incorrect" lead going around a turn, he has to work extra hard to bring his canter stride through, each step of the way.

Some horses break to a trot because they simply can't maintain the gait while on the outside lead.

Some horses have an easier time and just keep going, getting more strung out and unbalanced, but somehow sticking with the canter gait despite the imbalance. If your horse is one of these, you might have a harder time figuring out if he's in the correct lead or not.

What Is A Canter Lead?

Simply put, the horse will always "lead" with one hip and shoulder ahead of the other while in canter. So if he is on the "right" lead, his right hip and shoulder will be ahead of the left. We often teach beginner riders to look down at the shoulders to identify which shoulder is leading. Over time, you can learn to feel without looking at all.

The lead is caused not by the front legs, but by the hind legs. If you break down the canter stride, the *outside* hind leg is the first strike off leg. So, the left hind leg starts off the sequence of footfalls that allow the right hind leg and the right shoulder to lead. This is why we use our outside leg as the initiator of the canter gait.

Which Lead Is The "Correct" Lead?

If you are going right, the right lead is the "correct" lead. If you're going left, the left lead is "correct".

But here's the thing. I've used quotations on "correct" and "incorrect" because really, those are just definitions of sorts. We define the left lead as "incorrect" when the horse is going right. But it's "correct" when the horse is going left. So it's easy to see that the horse may choose either lead, depending on his balance mostly, unless he is well versed in responding to your leg aids.

As you both progress, you might one day purposely ask for the "incorrect" lead to get a counter canter. The counter canter is a great exercise in suppleness which helps develop hind end strength and flexibility.

Kathy Farrokhzad

The right hind is the "strike off" leg in this case – it's the first step of the left lead canter.

It also is a way to demonstrate that both the horse and rider can in fact pick up whichever lead in whichever direction - showing that the horse's balance is good enough to allow for either lead at any time.

So really, the "correct" lead might change meaning over time. But for the purposes of this article, we'll stick with "correct" meaning the same lead as the direction of movement.

What If Things Go Wrong?

As previously mentioned, "incorrect" leads happen all the time, especially during the developing stages of the horse or rider. The gait might be asked for at the wrong moment in time by the rider, and the educated horse will just follow by taking the opposite lead. In this case, the rider has to learn the correct timing of the aid to get the desired canter lead.

Alternately, the horse might be in the learning phases and might not know to respond promptly even if the rider's timing and aids are correct. In this case, he might not recognize the rider's outside leg as asking for the strike off, trot through the aid and strike off with the inside hind leg, again causing the counter canter.

Fix the Lead

There is a golden rule to stick to when things get discombobulated.

Secret: Slow down that trot!

Chances are, after you got the wrong lead, your horse eventually broke into an unbalanced trot (or you asked him to go back to the trot). In either case, this trot will likely be fast, on the forehand, and difficult to ride.

Your job at that moment is to be the creator of balance. Keep asking the horse to slow down in that trot. Wait for him to "come back under you" - so that he isn't running out while you just try to hang on. There is no point in asking the horse to try to canter on even while he's barely keeping balance in the trot.

So wait for him. Take your time. Teach him that there's no panic even after that uncomfortable canter thing just happened. It's all good!

Wait.

But here's the clincher. As soon as he's balanced, calm and ready - go! Be sure your aids are crystal clear - exaggerate the "windshield wiper" action of your outside leg.

If he only speeds up again in the trot, bring him back to that nice, slower tempo. Under all circumstances, don't kick him faster faster and "hope" he canters off. (There is one exception: while training the young horse, you should accept whatever he offers at the very beginning.)

Some horses can in fact canter out of an awkward trot, but invariably, that canter will be similarly hard to maintain. Always balance the trot before asking for the canter again.

27. WHAT TO DO WHEN YOUR HORSE PULLS

First off, let's be clear on the definition: if there is any pulling going on, it's the rider's responsibility! So even if you are convinced that the horse is the one who is pulling on the reins - either forward and down, or sideways away from a turn - the pulling is happening because you probably don't want to, or can't, let go. Or the horse is off balance and there's something you are doing, or *aren't* doing, to allow it to happen.

It is a good thing to look at the problem from the perspective that it is you who is pulling. Then, you can do something about it. "Pulling" is something that is absolutely under your control and something you can change if you focus on your aids and timing.

Break It Down

There are usually four reasons for pulling.

1) The horse is on the forehand.

A horse that is moving heavy on the front legs is going to be heavy on the reins. Kinder horses learn to brace in their jaws and necks and work through the increased pressure with little complaint on their parts. Less tolerant horses might slow their legs, alter their rhythm or balk to the pressure. You might notice ear pinning, teeth grinding or tail swishing at times.

Tension appears in both the horse and rider, even if it doesn't look like there is a lot of pressure on the reins. What happens is that the rider feels increased tension on the reins and many bear that weight through their arms, shoulders and backs. The tension becomes evident in tighter, more jarring movement. You might notice your hands bouncing or your seat leaving the saddle. Your legs might sway back and forth especially in the canter.

2) The horse is moving too slow.

The slow-moving horse is often on the forehand by virtue of lack of hind end engagement. Just because he takes shorter strides, or feels less bouncy because of less movement through the body, doesn't mean that he is moving well. These horses often become dull or "feel like cardboard" especially when it comes to responding to the reins. The back might feel long and flat as does the movement.

3) The horse is moving too fast.

The opposite can be the culprit as well. The horse that is moving too fast is automatically (or, biomechanically) put to the forehand and needs to brace his way to balance (to avoid a trip or fall). Once again, the weight on the reins are increased as the horse is put in the position of having too much weight to the front.

4) The rider initiates the pulling.

This happens to all of us, especially early in our riding career (but later on as well). We might even be unaware that we are doing the pulling ourselves. We are used to doing everything with our hands, so the first thing we do is grab for more pressure. Sometimes we pull back to counter our own falling-forward weight. Sometimes we want to influence the horse using more hands and not enough body. Finally, many of us just feel more confident with more pressure than is necessary - it's just hard to let go and be responsible for our own weight and balance.

Regardless of the reason *why* there is pulling going on, there is a four-step sequence of aids that might help you alleviate pressure on the reins and weight on the forehand. If you feel that your main problem is #4, additional work on developing your seat and core muscles might make a huge difference as well.

Here are the aids:

1. Give - only 1 inch.

Soften your elbows a tiny bit forward. Don't just open your fingers or let the reins out. Instead, control the rein length and actually advance both your hands forward, keeping the contact even and consistent.

Don't let the give be much more than that initially. It should be just enough to give the horse a feeling of freedom without being "thrown away" to the forehand.

If you are working on one side of the horse on a turn, you can give only the one elbow. If you are working straight ahead, you can give both elbows.

2. Activate with your seat and legs.

Some horses go with a forward thrust of just the seat bones. Other horses might need one or both legs (depending on the problem) to support the seat. In any case, you might feel a sudden surge in energy. Be ready and go with the movement. Make sure you don't get left behind when the horse responds with increased impulsion and maybe a larger stride length. This is especially useful for the pokey horses.

3. Finish with a half-halt.

Depending on the riding problem, you might want to use a half-halt or two after the moment of activation. If you allow the horse to lurch ahead with nothing to contain the energy at the end, the horse may fall to the forehand or just speed up. Always use a half-halt to "recycle the energy" and help the horse develop a more uphill balance. This is especially important for the horses that are too fast.

4. Take the reins back.

This last step is key. The idea isn't to just lengthen the rein out a little at a time, because that will only help your horse get longer and flatter and more strung out. So after you give a little, take a little. Keep the rein length essentially the same but do the give and take mainly through your elbows. If you do give rein length, this is the time to shorten the reins again.

End with what you started, only hopefully, this time, there is less pressure because the horse was given some freedom, some "oomph" and then some re-balancing. Remember that we are always working toward consistency - that is, we don't want to lengthen the reins, shorten the reins, move left or right, etc. In our dreams, we want to do as little as possible and look as quiet as possible.

28: COLLECTION: A BEGINNING EXERCISE TO TRY

I made a fairly bold statement long ago about differentiating between frame, roundness and collection. I said that most of us don't actually ride in collection with our horses, even when we think that's what we're doing.

I still stand by that comment, especially because there are a couple of misconceptions about what collection really means.

The Misconceptions

Collection isn't only about being slow. Many people think that if they slow down their horses (think disengagement of the hind end), that they are "collecting". It is true that upper level horses don't move their legs quickly, but the slowness doesn't come about because of lack of forward. In fact, it's quite the opposite. If the horse needs to elevate the legs higher, then he needs more time to do that. The legs move slower to allow for the increased "joint articulation" and movement required in collection.

Collection isn't about shortening the stride length either. People often think that if they can get their horses to travel over less ground, that they're collected. In fact, the leg *activity* increases. Although the horse takes more steps in less space, the energy goes into forming higher and rounder leg movement rather than just moving ahead over ground.

This is how I explained collection in the article:

> *In dressage, collection is the highest level of training for the horse. In other words, travelling while collected is difficult and requires a sophisticated level of balance, mental/emotional control, and understanding from the horse. The collected horse has developed the strength to tilt the haunches so the hind legs are far underneath the body, and the front end (head and neck included) is at the highest point. The horse moves in an "uphill" manner.*

Collection is achieved primarily by the seat and legs. The hands are the last to act, and ideally, serve to "catch and recycle" the energy produced by the seat and legs. The horse is not kept in place – the collected appearance is the result of the activity of the hind end. Let go of both reins, and the horse should stay in collection for several strides.

In The Beginning

Collection is difficult for both rider and horse to achieve, especially in the beginning, because of the re-definition of aids that needs to take place. While the horse and rider are in the novice stage of riding, leg aids can be used to just move into a gait, or to perform a transition.

But when you start working on collection, you will change your seat and leg aids to mean something different. In this case, leg aids need to mean "engagement" rather than just "go". Your expectation, as the rider, is that the horse puts more energy into the movement, without going bigger or faster or longer or changing gaits. In fact, your leg and seat aids combined will be morphing into something new to tell the horse: put more energy into your movement, reach deeper underneath your body, and begin to tilt your pelvis so that you can start to *carry* rather than *push*.

An Exercise

There is a (seemingly) simple exercise you can use to start to teach you and your horse what collection feels like. It can help your horse begin to feel what it's like to reach under with the hind legs and tilt the pelvis (even if just a little). It basically puts you into "assuming the position" rather than trying to force anything.

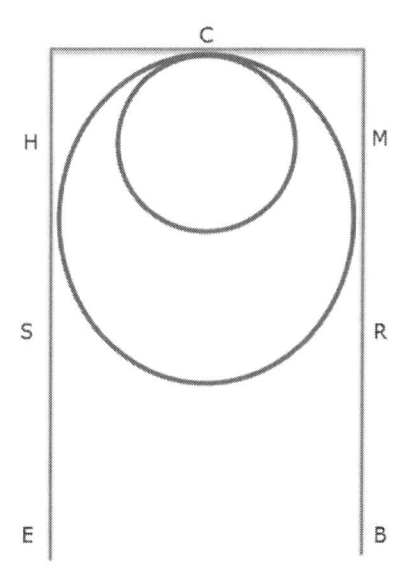

These are called "nested circles." The trick is that they both should start at the exact same point. So if you start the large circle at C, but then go into the small circle three-quarters into the circle, you'll lose the purpose of the exercise. Make sure you start them at the same place.

Do the large circle first. I have it drawn here at 20 metres, but you can adjust the size according to your riding space. The key is to make it large and evenly round. Take the opportunity here to activate your horse's hind legs.

You only need a mild bend, so although you want flexion (the horse looks in the direction of the turn), you can keep the horse fairly straight and focus on energy and activity. Make the strides large, find your ideal tempo and stay at that tempo, and then focus on the accuracy of the circle.

Then do the small circle. In the diagram, it's a 10-metre circle but again, you can play with the size a bit. Just don't make it too large, nor too small. You need it small enough to ask for a fairly deep bend, but not so small that your horse has trouble negotiating the turn in the first place.

Bend! As you approach the small circle (in the last quarter of the large circle), apply your bend aids - inside leg at the girth, outside leg behind the girth, your core and shoulders turned to the middle of the circle, mild inside rein contact for flexion, outside neck rein for direction - and bend before you hit C again. Then, move into the 10-m circle.

The horse should now have a fairly deep bend in the hind end as well as the front end. But make sure he doesn't just fall to the inside. The image of "wrapped around your inside leg" works well here. Complete the 10-m circle.

But Don't Forget!

This is where we all fall apart a bit. We tend to flop - either to the inside of the turn, or in our seat. Stay tall, turn in but don't lean or collapse, and *keep riding*!

During the small circle, you need to focus on more than just bend. You also have to encourage the horse to maintain or even *increase* his energy level. You can accept a mildly slower tempo with the legs, but you can't let the energy dissipate. In fact, do everything you can to encourage your horse to stay in front of your leg especially in the small circle.

At first, you'll feel a bit like a teeter totter. You will ask your horse to go, and he'll go but fall to the forehand and begin to rush off. Half-halt and try again.

If you don't ask the horse to go, he might break gait or quit altogether. Or sometimes, you ask the horse to go and he just runs off.

Be patient through these tries. Both of you have to learn what it feels like to carry rather than to just push with the hind end. Both of you need to figure out how much energy you need to put in to maintain gait with more activity and roundness.

So listen carefully to your horse, and see how much go you need and how much half-halt you need to not let the energy just run off.

If you find yourself and/or your horse huffing and puffing after just a few tries - congratulations! You're on the right track. You'll both need to develop the stamina to keep moving in collection over a longer period of time.

If you feel like you're just going from "go" to "not go", then you're also on the right track. Over time, you'll be able to be more diplomatic in your aids and your horse will become better at keeping his own balance.

Give this a try. Did your horse step deeper on the smaller circle? Were you able to keep up the activity level while on the smaller circle? Did you have any difficulties?

29. THE BENEFITS OF CANTERING ROUND AND ROUND THE RING

O r straight on the trail! If your horse is safe and the trail is suited for a longer canter, by all means, try this in the great outdoors.

There is no greater feeling of cantering on - and on, and on. Although you probably ride the canter regularly in your daily rides, there is something different about "living in" (an expression I first heard from Robert Dover) canter until it becomes normal - and effortless.

Just like the other gaits, the canter offers both the horse and the rider many learning experiences. Although we often ride the three-beat gait during any given ride, chances are that you're in and out of it in less than a minute. Because even just one minute of consistent canter seems like an awfully long time when you aren't used to it!

So here is something to practice. If you think your horse is fit enough, go ahead and give this a try. After an adequate warm-up, head into the canter. And don't stop. You can even time it with a watch. Go long enough to start to find the benefits below, but not so long that you'll run your horse into the ground.

If your horse loses balance and falls out (without you asking for the downward transition), calmly regain your balance, put the trot back together, find your good trot rhythm, and head off into the canter once more. You can change leads through a simple change (through walk or trot) or flying change. Just be sure to pick up the new lead and continue on as if nothing happened.

Start with one minute in canter. Then as you and your horse get fitter over the next few weeks, go to two minutes non-stop, then three. As with anything else in riding, the more you canter, the more effortless it becomes.

As you and your horse continue along, you will both strengthen and let go of tension. But there are many more benefits to discover.

Balance and Coordination

Many horses don't expect to maintain the canter for very long. For that very reason, they learn to disengage in the hind end after several strides and get longer and longer and... trot!

If you work at maintaining the canter, the horse learns that he should stay active in the hind end in order to feel better balanced. He'll learn to respond better to your seat and leg aids. He'll develop that "oomph" that he needs to keep going.

A longer canter will also give your body a chance to develop balance. You'll negotiate through the energy surges and drops from your horse. Your core muscles will work longer and develop their own intricate contractions and releases that will help your body stay in the saddle and maneuver within the horse's movement.

As you move around the arena, you will go from straight lines to curves to turns and circles. Both of you will strengthen in your ability to work through these changes of balance if you just give yourself enough time to adapt.

Conditioning

When the horse canters, his breathing rhythm ties into the rhythm of the strides. Cantering long term develops the lungs and muscles, making for a workout that is quite different from the walk or trot.

Same goes for the rider. If you canter long enough, you get a nice core workout that you might feel the next day!

Breath Development

Since the horse can only breathe with the canter strides, he will learn to breathe every step. Some horses puff in rhythm with the strides - those horses have already learned to regulate their breath according to the movement.

You might notice your own improvement in breathing as well. Many riders can easily hold their breath for the duration of a few canter circles. But even at just one minute, your body needs to finally let go and take a breath! You will be forced to breathe if you can maintain the canter long enough. Once you know how to breathe, you will have an easier time breathing at any gait.

Equalizer

The horse that speeds up in the canter will have enough time to settle down and discover that he'll run out of steam if he keeps rushing. He'll likely soften through the body, slow a bit in rhythm, and find a happy place where he can just keep going, but at a nice controlled pace.

The horse that likes to quit will learn that he has to give a little more - and even more. Soon enough, he'll get used to giving more and will develop the balance and coordination needed to keep going.

Suppleness

Once the horse settles in the canter rhythm, his topline muscles will find a release and he'll develop a better swing within the movement. At the end of the canter session, you might discover that his back loosens in the trot as well. His longitudinal suppleness will develop seemingly on its own.

You will also benefit. Many of us freeze up at the idea of cantering (and not even know it). If you put your body in the situation, and keep it there for some time, your tension will slowly dissipate, especially as your muscles tire. Once the release happens, your body can work on maintaining better posture over the long term.

Of course, don't overdo it. Keep your horse's current fitness level in mind. If you do go for a whole minute, be sure to give your horse a nice walk break afterward so he can catch his breath. If your horse is fitter than that, find the "just enough challenge" point without pushing him beyond his ability. Always err on the side of caution when doing something new or difficult.

30. HOW A SIMPLE 1,2,1,2... CAN IMPROVE YOUR RIDE

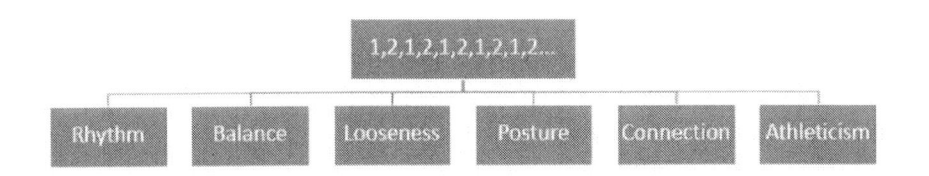

```
                    1,2,1,2,1,2,1,2,1,2...
   ┌──────┬──────────┬──────────┬──────────┬──────────┬──────────┐
 Rhythm  Balance  Looseness  Posture  Connection  Athleticism
```

HOW A SIMPLE

1,2,1,2,1,2...

CAN IMPROVE YOUR RIDE

It's such a simple thing that you might not think about it in the first place.

However, if you're a hunter/jumper, you might be absolutely familiar with it because you simply can't navigate through the jumps without doing it.

What is it?

Counting strides.

The difference between dressage counting and the jumping kind is that there is no jump to count up to. So it's easy to forget about it and just go along however things work out. But there's so much to be gained from the count!

All you have to do is count. 1,2,1,2,1,2... and so on, with each step of the front feet. You can count in all the gaits, in their own rhythm. But the 1,2... must stay consistent in each gait.

Of course, the tricky part is to get your horse to keep that *same* 1,2... in the gait. If you take some time to watch riders from the ringside, you might notice the tempo speed up and then slow down and then speed up again. The horse scrambles in speed, then quits through the turns or circles, then speeds up again when a leg aid is applied. Usually, the horse just goes along and the rider changes tempo to meet the horse's changes.

But the idea is to let the counting help you maintain tempo. Consistency is key for so many reasons!

How can counting the strides help? Here are five things that might improve for yourself and your horse.

Rhythm

First off, keeping a steady tempo will quite certainly help you maintain your horse's rhythm in each gait. Change of leg speed almost always throws the horse's weight to the forehand, and can cause variations in the footfalls. If you focus on tempo, your horse will have a better chance of maintaining "pure" gaits - that is, keeping a walk to an even 4-beat, keeping the trot to a consistent diagonal pair 2-beat, and the canter to a 3-beat with the moment of suspension.

So, the first focus of your count should be to ensure that the horse has an even and consistent rhythm at each gait. Feel for the strides and listen to the footfalls to gauge the quality of the rhythm.

Balance

Lack of tempo often causes balance changes in the movement. Have you ever felt like you were going just great at the trot and then suddenly there's a small whiplash dive to the forehand, then a sudden blocking of the energy? Your upper body falls first forward and then backward. The tossing around you feel is connected to balance changes as the horse also falls to the forehand or loses engagement.

Balance is the second almost natural result of the 1,2... count. When you stabilize the leg movement, the horse will have plenty of time for each leg to come through. This allows for a stronger and more consistent weight bearing from the hind end, which will allow the horse to keep better balance. You won't be flung around as much, and soon enough, you will both float along as if "one."

Looseness

As the horse relaxes in the gait, he will likely find more opportunity for "free movement." You might notice more bounce in his stride, more reach through the shoulders, and more swing through the back. To me, it feels like a trampoline. Beware! If you cannot become loose yourself and ride that motion, you will likely block your horse from continuing in this manner. So you have to feel for the looseness, recognize it and *ride it*!

Posture

Once you have a steady rhythm, consistent balance, and looseness, the horse's posture might just fall into place seemingly on its own. The back will rise and fall, the body will round and the horse will begin to tilt a little more in the hind end. Your horse's neck will assume a height that is natural to his conformation. No more high heads, no more diving down necks.

Connection

The next step is an improved sense of connectedness between the horse and rider. The horse may reach more for the bit. The rider might be able to keep her own balance better and therefore stay better with the horse's movement. There will now be an opportunity for the aids to become more subtle.

The communication will be much more pronounced and clear than it ever can be when the horse is inconsistent. This means less rein aids are needed even while the contact is improved.

Athleticism

Finally, you might notice an amazing increase in athletic ability, both from the horse and the rider. All it takes is a small change of aid for anything - downward transition, sharp turn, change of bend, lengthen. Any movement becomes easier because the basic balance is already in place. The horse is stronger, looser, and maybe slower than before - these will all contribute to better comfort in movement for both the horse and rider.

One last note: use the half-halt! Initially, keeping that absolutely consistent gait will likely be difficult. If you aren't used to counting strides, you will have to work hard to identify when the tempo speeds up and slows down. Then you will have to figure out how influence the horse to not let him rush but also not slow into disengagement. The half-halt is definitely an integral part of the puzzle.

Wow!

All this with a simple 1,2,1,2... count?

Try it and see what happens for you and your horse.

PARTING THOUGHTS

31. THREE RELAXING WAYS TO COOL DOWN AT THE END OF YOUR RIDE

What do you do towards the end of your ride? Do you find yourself hopping off shortly after you're done with the "lesson" part of your ride? It's tempting to do a few minutes of walking just to loosen your horse up a little and leave it at that. But do you know that there are many excellent exercises you can use to cool off and also build on your skills and communication with your horse?

If you can make these exercises a part of your routine, you might be pleasantly surprised at how easily your horse will pick up the new skills, and how the repetition will help you in your position and use of the seat and legs. The more you practice, the easier the movements will become, and practicing them at the walk will set you and your horse up for having an easier time transitioning to the trot and canter.

Doing these exercises at the walk will give you time to better use your aids. They will also give your horse time to learn to respond. It's a win-win all around, and adding them to the tail end (pun!) of your ride on a regular basis will ensure that you actually do devote enough time to make good progress.

Leg Yield to the Rail

This one is a very basic movement that you can teach young and uneducated horses.

Come off the rail just after the letter C or A and head in a straight line parallel to the rail. Now apply your inside leg and ask your horse to step forward-sideways back to the rail. Be sure to keep the horse's body straight while you step sideways, as walking back to the rail in a diagonal line isn't a leg yield. Keep even weight on your seat bones.

You can have the horse flexed slightly to the outside (so you can see the corner of the horse's outside eye) but the neck should be straight. If the horse leans one way or the other, just abort the leg yield, re-establish your good walk, then try again.

Walk Up Center Line and Halt, Back and Walk

First off, walking a straight line without any walls to help you might be challenging enough. Then, practice halting. You can halt at different spots on the line each time, so the horse doesn't learn to anticipate. Ideally, you will use very little rein (half-halt preferred) and the horse should stop when your seat stops. Then count to 5 while standing still. Keep your reins straight and "on" because you will back up in a moment.

After a stationary halt, apply your legs as you continue to hold the reins. The horse should give a forward-inclination before heading backwards in diagonal pairs of legs. Lighten your seat bones just a bit (not enough for an onlooker to see the difference in your posture) to invite the horse to use his back. Halt again after a designated number of steps (4 or 6 steps should be fine).

Then walk on. Make sure your new walk is straight and active. Continue until the end of the ring and turn.

Medium Walk-Stretchy Walk-Medium Walk

This movement occurs in many of the dressage tests but aside from preparing for shows, it's one of my favorite ways to teach the horse to swing through the back and then keep that loose back while re-establishing contact.

Start with medium walk. Come off the rail at the corner and head across the diagonal to change directions. Maintain an active walk, and use your seat to ask the horse to take the reins out of your hands. Note that you don't give the reins to the horse, but vice versa. The horse should stretch his neck down, head out and keep marching on in a forward striding, ground covering walk. Feel for the "trampoline" feeling of the swing of the back.

Then a few strides before the end of the diagonal, pick up the reins again, establish contact and keep marching. See if you can keep the swing you established during the stretch, even though the horse's outline is shorter now. Horses will often slow down or back off the bit as contact is being taken up, so it takes quite a lot of practice to teach the horse to walk into the contact and stay active through the corner.

I hope these three exercises will give you some structured ideas to add to your ride. If you do each of these exercises a few times each way, you can add 10 minutes or more to your ride, at the walk, allowing the horse to cool down physically and cool off mentally. They will also add a repertoire of skills and increase communication between you and your horse.

Have fun!

32. THE DIFFERENCE BETWEEN RHYTHM AND TEMPO

Confused about which is which? Do you use them interchangeably sometimes? I did, until I finally figured out the difference. Although I've already had a good grasp of rhythm and tempo in musical arrangements, it took some time for me to extrapolate that understanding and apply it to horse riding.

☑ **Rhythm**

☑ **Tempo**

Rhythm

When it comes to horses, rhythm refers to the number of beats in a horse's gait. So for example, a walk is a four-beat gait. A trot is two beats (diagonal pairs fall together) and a canter is 3 beats (outside hind, diagonal pair, and inside front, suspension). Because the canter has that moment of suspension, you hear only three footfalls with a quiet moment in between.

The rhythm of the gait is non-negotiable. That is, a canter *must* have three footfalls and a moment of suspension, while a trot must have two. Problems arise when the horse demonstrates what is called an "impure" or "irregular" gait.

Let's say you are trotting along and you hear four beats per stride, something like a thud-thud-thud-thud in quick succession. This indicates that the trot is not in rhythm. If you were on the ground watching, you might even be able to see the legs hitting the ground at different moments. It happens quickly but a practiced eye can see it.

More often, we see horses four-beating the canter. Rather than maintaining the diagonal pair of legs for the second beat, the horse lands those legs in a one-two fashion - which results in four independent footfalls.

In both cases, the rhythm needs to be maintained. Chances are, the horse needs more impulsion, especially in turns or changes of bend. It is also possible that the irregularity stems from a physical discomfort, so you may want to call a vet to make sure there is no unsoundness.

There is one exception to these rules: the gaited horse.

Many horses have been bred over generations to produce distinct 4-beat gaits specific to their bloodlines. For example, the Tennessee Walking Horse is famous for its running walk. These horses *shouldn't* move in two beats in these gaits. The four-beat is the rhythm of the gait.

When working on any particular gait, you must maintain the rhythm of that gait. So if your horse four-beats the canter, you probably need to ask for better impulsion and engagement of the hind end, and find those 3-beats.

First, work on getting and maintaining distinct rhythmical footfalls.

Tempo

Once you can keep a consistent rhythm, the next area to focus on is the tempo, otherwise known as the horse's leg speed. Tempo is the second priority only after the rhythm has been established. Incorrect tempo is possibly more difficult to recognize and correct than rhythm.

Think of tempo as the speed of the footfalls. You could be in a two-beat trot, but how *fast* you go would be due to how quickly the legs land on the ground. You can imagine that there are many tempos within one gait. So a trot may be two beats, but how quickly the horses move in those two beats can be dependent on the horse's breed and conformation, and the rider's skills.

Many of us are prone to letting the horse (or sometimes actually "chasing" the horse) move into a too-quick tempo, which can result in the horse falling to the forehand, or even breaking stride. We get into a frantic one-two rising trot that speeds up the horse, which then speeds up our posting, which then speeds up the horse even more....

You get the idea. We end up in a never-ending cycle of speed and eventually it feels "normal" to rush along on the forehand, using the rail to keep the horse from drifting out too far.

The opposite can happen too, although not quite as often. If we work at slowing the tempo down to point that the horse loses energy, we run the risk of breaking rhythm. This is often why horses four-beat in the trot or canter. Too slow without additional energy can be as detrimental as too fast.

Try This

Listen carefully to your horse's footfalls as you ride at each gait. Every horse has an ideal tempo that allows him to work with adequate energy - but not too much - so he does not lose balance.

Your horse's best leg speed is probably slower than you think. But you can try an experiment. Increase the leg speed in a particular gait and feel for your horse's threshold. At some point, your horse suddenly feels like he has to scramble to keep his legs underneath him.

Then do the opposite. Slow the legs to just before the point that your horse is going to quit. Maintain energy and see if he can soften through the body and breathe in better rhythm. Too slow, and he will likely break stride. But slow and strong might be just what he needs.

The ideal tempo allows the horse to move with less tension in better balance and in a steady, true rhythm. There is no speeding up or slowing down every few strides. Each step is deliberate and well placed. There is a sense of strong but calm energy from both horse and rider.

You can try this exercise several times. It doesn't hurt for the horse to know what it feels like to increase and decrease the tempo in a gait. In fact, it might help as he progresses into more collected work. But in the meantime, remember that rhythm must be maintained while tempo can be adjusted.

33. WHY BORING IS BEAUTIFUL IN HORSE BACK RIDING

They say horseback riding, especially "flat work" is boring. It's like watching paint dry.

It's true that there is little excitement to be seen when the horse moves in a steady tempo, glides through the gait changes, and seems to be doing everything on his own volition. It's pretty dull to watch the rider that appears to be doing absolutely nothing other than staying on top of the horse.

Bucks and rears? None.

Harsh riding? Nope.

Now I'm not talking about the kind of boring that you might see if someone just sits on the horse and does nary a thing at all. That can, in fact, be quite boring.

This kind of boring requires movement. You go places. The horse floats and glides. The rider is so quiet that we forget that she's there. The transitions happen, the figures come one after the other in perfect succession. While there is definite communication happening, it's subtle and refined.

This is the kind of boring that excites the educated observer. In fact, it is within all the calmness that one can see the true togetherness of the horse and rider. The respect and the compassion goes both ways. This is the stuff of dreams, the quiet that inspires and exhilarates the people who really know what they're seeing.

Why Is Boring Beautiful?

Harmony

The opposite of conflict is harmony. In the riding sense, the horse and rider seem to connect in a way that allows them to "become one." While there is plenty of activity and movement, there is little stop-and-go, and rare bobbles. Negative tension in terms of pinned ears, gaping mouth, and tight back are not apparent.

Freedom of Movement

The horse just flows. The shoulders reach, the body is round and the movement is bouncy. It looks effortless and powerful at the same time. The lack of conflict gives the rider so much more time to devote to staying with the horse, communicating and *riding*.

Confidence

Both horse and rider seem at ease with each other. They can afford to trust in a way that results in a bold way of going that cannot happen if there is tension involved. The horse is allowed to be expressive and take initiative while the rider quietly stays in the movement.

Communication

Boring simply can't happen without a sophisticated level of communication. As soon as the "conversation" breaks down, there will be tension and all the associated problems. Of course, developing a language between horse and rider takes time and education on both parts. Therefore, you might notice your rides becoming more "boring" as you both become experienced in knowing what to do when.

Compassion

There is a certain amount of care and attention that goes into a nice boring ride! Compassion comes in many forms. It is not necessary to be harsher in your aids when something doesn't work out - just take a moment to regroup and try it again. Appreciate the horse's efforts. Be encouraging, speak in a kind voice.

Certainty

There's something purposeful about a pair that is moving together, in confidence, with that subtle communication. It looks like they both know where they are going, what they are doing, and what's coming next. There is no confusion or discord between them.

All of these intangible qualities combine to make the overall picture of the horse and rider a thing of beauty. More importantly, the true beauty lies in the positive experience for both.

To those that walk away: you can keep your exciting rides - I'm going to work on boring!

34. "YOU'RE STILL TAKING RIDING LESSONS?"

Maybe you've heard that question more frequently than you'd like to. It happens all the time to us lifelong horse owners and riders. Surely, after all these years, you should know everything there is to know! Think of everything you've done with your horse. How can there possibly be more for you to learn?

This is especially for those who have been riding for years and years. Do your friends insinuate that there might be something wrong with you if you *still* need lessons after all this time? Do your parents, friends, significant other complain that you shouldn't need to go to that clinic since you can pretty much write the book by yourself?

It's hard to put into words how there is no such thing as knowing *everything* in horse riding, that levels of expertise are relative and there's always more and more and more.... If there ever were an embodiment of life-long learning, horse riding is it!

Quick Fixes

As an instructor, when I start lessons with a new (lifelong) rider, two things happen. There is an initial change during the first few months, but the real learning takes a lot longer.

The little nit-picking bad habits that we can address right away will generally make an initial positive impact on the rider's feel and the horse's way of going. These fixes will make an obvious difference if practiced consistently during homework rides because they are likely the quick fixes that are currently getting in your (horse's) way.

They are the ones that are easier to do because they require less coordination or build on what you already have achieved.

The Plateau

Then invariably, the plateau hits. While it seems that nothing really changes during this stage, it is an essential part of long-term development. This is where the tough learning happens, where we work on firmly entrenched muscle memory habits that prevent progress. This is when you wonder if taking those lessons really make any difference at all!

Sometimes you have to take a few steps back to step ahead.

Real Change

Making significant change can take at least 2 years - usually more if you take lessons (= get reinforcement) only once a week. Getting to the root of a problem is a difficult task not only in terms of changing old habits but also in terms of blueprinting new responses and movements.

We usually need to work on our basic skills more than anything. This is because all the more advanced movements rely on sound basics. Once you move on to the higher level movements, problems will arise not from the highest level skills, but from the basic skills that have not been established enough to be able to support the higher skills.

For example, you might be working on more advanced movements such as shoulder-in or half-pass when you discover that you have to give up the laterals *yet again* to better establish forward movement and straightness. Or how about the time when you think you're already sitting well in trot only to realize that you have to be more toned - which requires much more lower abdominal and core muscles than you're used to? Those changes seem to take much effort and time.

Little by little, you whittle away at the old habits, establish new habits, and build upon correct learning. Yes, this takes years, especially if you didn't start with strong basics in the first place.

But by then, the change is surely substantial because you would have made many small but significant changes to your basic skills that not only make your own riding better, but change your horse's life. There is nothing more satisfying than to one day realize your horse is moving stronger and more freely than ever before because of your dedication to making those changes in your own riding - day in, day out - until you can finally see and feel the result in your horse.

35. 10 SYMPTOMS OF A HORSE-A-HOLIC

Are you a horse-a-holic - the kind of horse lover that makes horses a lifestyle, not just a hobby?

You know what I mean. First you were the horse lover. Then you became the horse rider. Maybe then you turned into a horse keeper - who then ended up living, breathing, smelling, *being* (well, especially during shedding season) horses. The official recognition of "horse-a-holic" requires many achievements beyond just loving horses and thinking they're cute. You have to earn your way into that elite category!

Take a look at the following symptoms and see how many apply to you!

1. Do you apply almost every concept to something about horses?

It can be anything and everything and doesn't need to have any resemblance to horses - but you'll find a way! Figure skating informs your understanding about core and balance - which of course, you need to be able to ride well. Music must be analyzed to decide if it would match a walk, trot or canter rhythm. "Soft eyes" can help you not only in the riding ring, but out on the road as well, as you change lanes and maneuver between vehicles.

2. Do you notice how so many ladies' tall boots are riding boot imitations?

You find it alternately pleasing and irritating that the new "tall boot" fashion boots look like riding boots. On the one hand, you love the decorative hardware and straight-bottomed heel (in case you ever want to wear that boot to actually ride). On the other hand, it displeases you that almost *everybody* is wearing some version of your show riding boot - and not riding at all!

3. Does your Facebook page have more horsey pics than human pics?

This is a key indicator of your horse-a-holic-ness. Take a small unbiased survey of your recent timeline. How many of your posts have something in them about horses or riding? Do you share hilarious horsey memes more often than not? Are your friends and otherwise non-horsey humans relegated to only the odd post and picture?

4. Without thinking about it, do you move people around with the same body language that you use to move horses around?

Hey, it works! It's easy, effective, efficient and best of all, no one knows you're doing it!

5. Do you mistakenly cluck at people (and then look away and pretend the sound came from somewhere else)?

This one can be a bit embarrassing but the real truth is that you don't do it on purpose. It's like your clucking machine just takes over and you've clucked before you even knew you were doing it.

6. Do you have to actually think about *not* calling "door" when entering... your office?

This one takes quite a bit of effort, especially if you are at a barn that requires you to use your voice at every entrance and exit. Once you get into the swing of it, you might find it very difficult to hold back at any doorway. Which then can lead to interesting and confused glances in your direction.

7. Have you become picky about the amount of "denier" and "fill" you want for your horse's blankets?

You have become quite the expert at identifying quality of horse blanket fabric and you know exactly how much thickness your horse needs for which weather conditions.

8. Do you pre-book tickets to the horsey event of the year - and invariably, max out on the group size limit (so some of your barn friends end up being left out)?

It happens every year but you're bound and determined to get that row of tickets no matter what happens! You'll stay up late or get up early so you can be one of the first to get on that ticket selling website.

9. Can you throw around the terms "aught", "1 degree", "contracted" and "laminae" with the best of them - and actually know what you're talking about?

There's nothing like being a lifelong learner, and knowing all about your horse's feet fits the description perfectly. No hoof, no horse, as they say - and so you learn everything there is about hoof physiology, mechanics and maintenance. Plus you know quite well that your farrier really is your horse's best friend.

10. Do you get irritated when your well-meaning non-horsey friends post a horse pic on your Timeline - the one you already saw months ago and decided NOT to share?

Well, honestly, it's because you've seen them all, as soon as they came out. So if you didn't share it, it wasn't worthy!

So how did it go? Are you a full-on horse-a-holic, or just a wannabe?

36. THE TRUTH ABOUT PERFECT PRACTICE AND THE HL RIDER LEARNING CYCLE

Hands up if you feel you're *ever* perfect while you ride! I bet even our best international riders would agree that there's always something to develop, something to improve, a more subtle aid, a quieter seat, a more harmonious movement.

"Practice doesn't make perfect. Perfect practice makes perfect."

Even Vince Lombardi himself, who is often quoted as the originator of the above quote, qualified his statement by saying, "Perfection is not attainable but if we chase perfection, we can catch excellence." This makes much more sense to me.

So how does perfect practice relate to us non-Olympic-bound, job-and-family-restricted, ride-only-a-few-times-a-week riders?

I have a theory. But perfection is only a tiny part of it.

The Horse Listening Rider Learning Cycle
Start at the bottom.

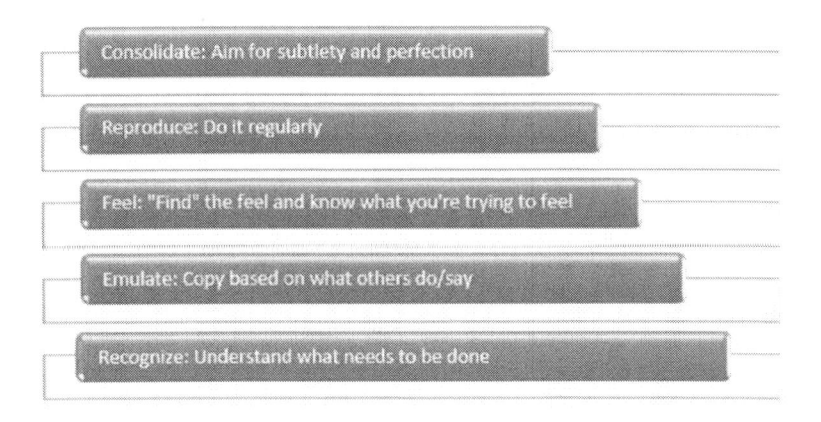

- Consolidate: Aim for subtlety and perfection
- Reproduce: Do it regularly
- Feel: "Find" the feel and know what you're trying to feel
- Emulate: Copy based on what others do/say
- Recognize: Understand what needs to be done

This learning scale is based purely on personal observation. There have been no formal studies done! However, I can tell you as an educator and a riding instructor *and* as a riding *student* that most people go through similar phases as they work their way toward "perfection." Let's break it down.

1. Recognize

This is the first part of any learning. Before you know something, you have to begin to recognize it in the first place. This is what "developing your eye" is all about. As you learn more about riding and the intricate nuances that go into each movement, you'll be able to observe little things that other people might completely miss. For example, can you actually identify the moment a rider applies a half-halt? Do you know the difference between a "good" trot and a "not as good" trot?

2. Emulate

Once you know what you're looking for, you will have a better idea on what you need to do.

While you may be able to see what is happening from the ground, it is entirely another thing to be able to do it in saddle. At this stage, you are probably putting a lot of effort into your tries, and making a lot of mistakes. Trial and error is exactly what should be happening at this stage (please apologize to your horse as needed).

3. Feel

This is when things get exciting! Those first "feels" are golden moments, especially because suddenly everything comes together and you momentarily float together with your horse in an effortless cloud of movement.

Then it all falls apart!

This is normal too. After you know what you are feeling for, you will be inspired to try, try again to find it again. You'll do it until you think you have it, then lose it again, only to find it even better and more confidently as time goes on.

4. Reproduce

Sometimes sooner, sometimes later, you'll suddenly realize that you can in fact get what you want - quite well, almost all the time! This is when you've learned something so well that you can do it on different horses, under different circumstances (shows or clinics, anyone?) and in front of an all-knowing audience (but you feel confident enough, thank-you-very-much).

This is the stage where you feel so established that you might not want to get out of your comfort zone anymore. I think this is where many of us end our learning journeys simply because everything comes fairly easily and we're safe much of the time.

5. Consolidate

This stage is for the lifelong learners. It's for the perfectionists. It's also for those aspiring riders who do want to perform at the highest level that they can.

This is also where I believe "perfect practice" comes into the scheme of things.

Have you ever done something a million times, only to find a deeper, clearer or better understanding in the million-and-first time? This is the consolidation stage.

You're already fluid, fluent, utterly comfortable - but suddenly, you learn something that changes your whole understanding and/or feel. Just when you think you know it all, you discover how much more there is to learn. But because of your already impeccable skills, you can and should refine, reduce, become more subtle, be more effective, move less... and still work to you and your horse's highest potential.

You can't really get to this stage *without* aiming for perfection. Even while the concept of perfection might be different between person to person, or within differing riding disciplines, being able to do something really well *over and over again* is an art to itself indeed.

♦ ♦ ♦

I call it a learning "cycle" because I believe that each and every skill you develop goes through these learning stages over and over again. Every time you learn something new, you start at the bottom and work your way to the top.

Perfect practice is not something we can start at the beginning of the learning cycle. We can only begin to perfect our skills once we've achieved a certain level of accomplishment. And in the end, especially in horse riding, I think it's better to think to work toward *excellence* - not perfection. Because such a thing surely does not exist.

37. TWENTY-FOUR REASONS WHY HORSIN' AROUND MAKES US BETTER HUMAN BEINGS

I often write about how being around horses changes a person. In many ways, there is no chance that a person who is involved in horses - whether as a rider, or barn owner or manager, instructor, volunteer, or someone who helps with the chores - can stay the same as they were pre-horses. While there's likely plenty of physical improvement, there's the even more important aspect of development of character.

Well, it makes sense when you think about it.

First off, there's the being-out-in-the-country factor. For many of us who live in suburbs or cities, being outside "for real" puts us in a much different position than we're used to. The sheer space and conditions create an environment that is rarely experienced these days by most people. Quite opposite to the hustle and bustle of our city lives, being at a farm makes us do things differently.

Time slows down. Pace slows down. Even while we have to actually perform tasks (that won't get done otherwise), the physical aspect requires us to focus on one thing at a time, prioritize tasks, find the most efficient way to do things and to "live in the moment."

Then there's the horses.

They teach us so many "soft" skills like empathy, responsibility, leadership, compassion, determination and organization. That doesn't even include riding-specific skills.

So why does horsin' around make us into better human beings? Here are 24 ways.

Work hard: Whether we're carrying water buckets or cleaning out stall after stall, we're in it to get 'er done, no matter what it takes!

Ready to pitch in when needed: We learn quickly that many hands make light work.

Compassion - for people too: (As in, not only for the animals. We become "tuned in" to others, period.)

Clean without complaint: Well, maybe just a little complaint. But we realize that if we don't do the cleaning, the mess will build up quickly and not go away on its own!

Walk briskly and far: Walking is the major way to get around farms and so you learn to go - fast!

Not afraid to get dirty: We get right into the mess of things and clean up later.

Keep doing despite the weather: Like turning horses in just as the huge downpour begins, or taking the wheelbarrow to the muck pile after a white-out blizzard covers the path.

Put others' needs first: The horses always get taken care of first because they rely on us for almost everything.

Stubborn: In a good way, we try, try again in order to learn the new skill.

Make decisions - even the hard ones: As the person responsible for the horse, it's our duty to keep our selfish needs to the side and do what's best for the horse.

Have fun! Stay a while in any barn and hear the laughter echo through the rafters (literally).

Alone time: Except we're not really alone. We relish our quiet time listening to the munching of hay and occasional snorts of our equine friends.

Enjoy being with others: Even the most introverted of us becomes more outgoing and social simply by virtue of the shared passion we have for horses.

Stick to it when the going gets tough: We learn that almost any problem can be overcome with perseverance and a little bit of creativity.

Willing to "perform" in front of others: There's no way around it. You watch others ride and others watch you ride.

Step out of own comfort zone regularly: We become more willing to do try new things and grow - whether in the saddle or on the ground.

Share information and knowledge with others: We pool together all of experiences and research especially when there's a horse in need.

Finish tasks: Because the chore won't get done otherwise.

Take initiative: Our leadership skills flourish in a barn setting.

Lift heavy objects: We build our strength and we aren't shy to use it (water bucket, anyone)?

Can be counted on to pitch in or complete tasks: Because that's just the way things get done in a barn.

Communicate clearly: We use white boards, lists, text messages, memos, and old fashioned "face time" to make sure we're on track and the horses are taken care of in a consistent manner.

Self-starters: We will find the things that need to be done and do them on our own.

Life-long learners: Because we need more than one lifetime to learn everything we need to know about riding and horses.

When you take a look at those 24 characteristic traits, it's pretty easy to realize that little by little, day by day, being out in that barn and interacting with those horses adds a huge dimension to our way of being in the world. How have your horses made you into a better human being?

ABOUT THE AUTHOR

Kathy Farrokhzad is the author of Horse Listening Book Collection, and other books. She is internationally published in national equine magazines and has a monthly column in The Rider. She is also owner and writer of the blog, www.horselsistening.com.

An Equine Canada Competition Coach, she has taught beginner to intermediate students for over 20 years. She has worked with all types of horses in a showing, riding, training and teaching capacity in several disciplines.

Kathy practices what she preaches. Her writing reflects her experiences as a coach, trainer and rider. She has used all of the exercises in this book previously for her students, their horses, and horses she rides.

If you liked this book, be sure to visit her blog, HorseListening.com, for much more!

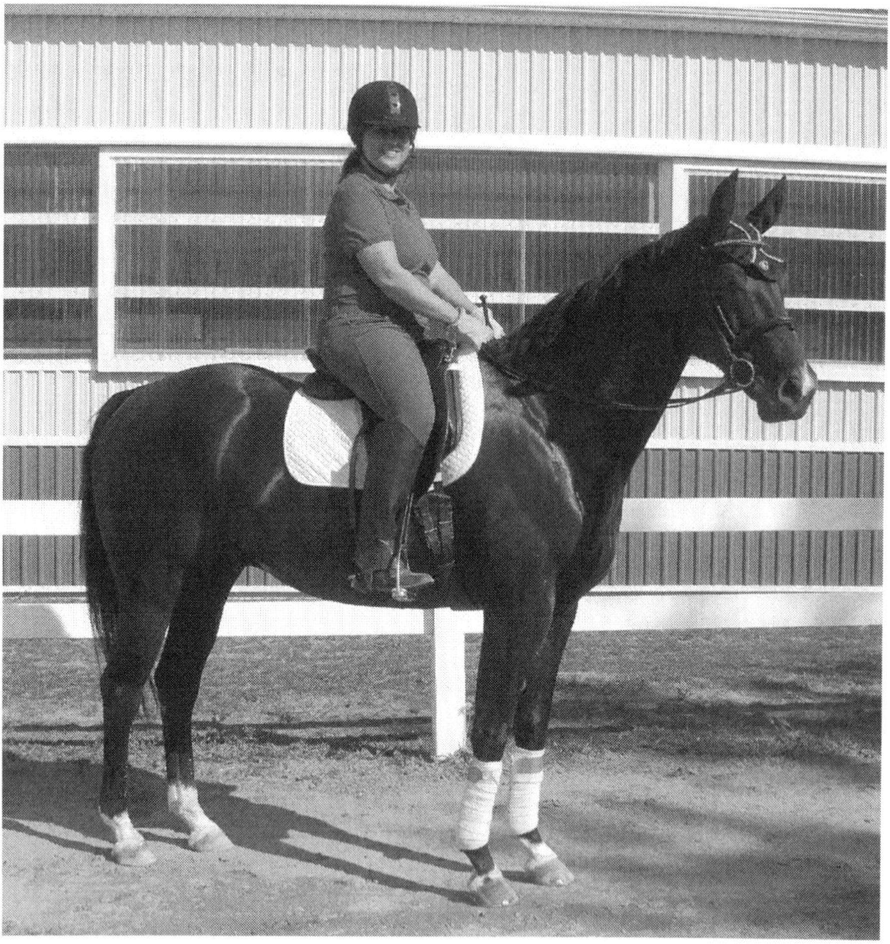

The Horse Listening Collection

Do you wish your horseback riding lessons could come with a user manual? Do you feel that you could serve your horses better as a rider if you only know how and what to do? Would you like to be the rider that all horses dream of?

The Horse Listening books focus specifically on riding as a means of improving the horse. Based on the popular blog, HorseListening.com, the exercises and ideas are purposely handpicked to help you develop your path to becoming an effective rider, not only for your own benefit, but also for your horse's long-term wellbeing. Each book has a particular focus. By following these simple, useful exercises, you will be able to develop a better understanding about the rider's aids, the use of the seat, balance, impulsion, bend and straightness, and much more.

Go to horselistening.com/book to see the specific focus of each book.

Goal Setting For the Equestrian: A Personal Workbook

> I find it really helpful to journal my lessons and my rides! It keeps me more focused while consciously giving my horse and I credit for the great strides we are making together! I'm ordering my 2nd workbook today!
> – Kris TwoOwls, 5* Amazon Review

Goal Setting For the Equestrian: A Personal Workbook is a guided planner that will help you devise your individualized goals and milestones. Fill in the pages as you chart your progress over the course of a year. Everything you need to keep track of the little steps and big milestones are here: - What rider improvement really means - The theory behind setting positive, realistic goals - Set S.M.A.R.T. goals as they relate to horses and riding - Long term planning - Short term planning - Journal style weekly entries - Special event debriefs.

This is a system designed specifically for horse people seeking self-improvement in any equestrian pursuit (not only riding related).

Printed in Great Britain
by Amazon